MOUNTAIN
JACK TALES

MOUNTAIN JACK TALES

as told and illustrated by
Gail E. Haley

2002

Parkway Publishers, Inc.
Boone, North Carolina

Available from:

Parkway Publishers, Inc.
P. O. Box 3678
Boone, North Carolina 28607
Telephone/Facsimile: (828) 265-3993
www.parkwaypublishers.com

Library of Congress Cataloging-in-Publication Data

Haley, Gail E.
    Mountain Jack tales / as told and illustrated by Gail E.Haley.
        p. cm.
    Summary: These stories featuring the hero Jack are set in the
    mountains of North Carolina, but have their roots in Old World
    folklore.
    ISBN 1-887905-51-0
    1. Jack tales--North Carolina. [1. Jack tales. 2. Folklore--North
    Carolina.] I. Title

PZ8.1.H139 Mo 2001
398.2'09756'02--dc21

2001037445

For Ray Hicks and all the members
of NAPPS, who keep sharing the stories

Contents

Introduction

There are many surprises in these mountains; the New River is one of the oldest in the world, running down between the ancient ranges peaceful and patient as old ladies candlewicking. Yet an ice storm or avalanche can carry away half of the mountain trees; a flash flood can destroy the puny houses, bridges, and even automobiles of humankind.

There is beauty to be found at every turn of the road: vistas of blue mountains stretching for miles; trees in the autumn sporting colors too vivid for human cameras or paintbrushes ever to duplicate; budding hillsides in spring as soft as rabbit fur.

Much has remained unchanged. Herds of wide-eyed deer

trip through the woods. The black bear still fishes in white water for dinner; fox kits cavort in the tall grass.

But over the years the tourists have come, for cool in summer's heat, for skiing in the winter. So highways have cut deeper into the mountains. Filling stations, grocery stores, ammunition shops, and flea markets dot the roads. There are stores with rubber Indians and chenille peacock bedspreads displayed beside mountain quilts. Inside, polyester coonskin caps and moccasins made in Taiwan are displayed for sale. It's hard to see a cabin or house from the road that doesn't have a TV antenna or satellite dish.

And yet, if you drive off the highway just a little piece, up a dirt road, past the granddaddy oak and the crooked persimmon tree, you can catch sight of a neat little cabin where woodsmoke curls up year-round. You can park your car and hike up the path to Poppyseed's house. You will be watched. Wood creatures and the pale eyes of things forgotten in the outside world will see your every move.

At Poppyseed's house, you'll leave your world behind and travel into country where there are still unicorns and dragons, witches, fairies, and mysterious wizards. You will find talking animals, magic spells, and a place where a hero can still win his silver sword and conquer giants.

The only price for all these treasures is that you may have to shuck a few ears of corn, peel some apples, or string some leather breeches for the winter while Poppyseed spins her tales.

MOUNTAIN JACK TALES

Poppyseed's Invitation

Well, howdy. Pull up a chair, and grab you-uns a knife and a pan. I've got to get these apples peeled and spread out to dry. Once fall comes on, and the clouds come creeping cold and gray over the mountains, there won't be enough sun to dry anything. I've got a mess of them in the kitchen, boiling down for apple butter. Before you leave, there'll be some to sample with biscuits and fresh-churned butter.

You look like someone who's come to hear a story. You're in the right place. This here mountain is called Story Mountain. We call it that because this is the very spot where Jack planted the three magic beans that grew into the bean tree.

3

The roots of that tree stretch down, down, down, into the heart of the Earth herself. They're down there, just whispering and talking—telling all the stories that ever were.

Often I think about them three beans that Jack got from Old Graybeard in exchange for Milky White the Cow. I get to wondering how they took Jack so far, and why you young-uns are always asking to hear that story. The way I see it, they are part of a riddle that's been around since the beginning of time. My granny had a china plate that come clear across the ocean and up to the mountains on a covered wagon. There was a design on it that finally helped me solve the riddle of the three beans. If I take three dried beans and put them down in a circle like this,

it'll help me explain what I think the answer is.

The first bean is Jack—the hero. He's the young feller who'll risk just about everything to have an adventure. It's like a hunger he has, and his dreams will lead him into places where an older, wiser person might think twice about goin'. Course, if he didn't start out in a foolhardy sort of way, he might not have the adventure.

It's believing and taking the chances that get him the beans. But it's losing everything and learning to cry that really set the beans a-growin'. And while his bean tree is there, he can climb up it to find food, money, and songs for his soul.

But it's Jack himself who must cut it down, else we'd have giants ravaging the countryside. The bad thing about that is that Jack lost the bean tree. The good thing is that the beans off that tree scattered every which way. And magic beans can last might nigh forever. A young-un never knows when one of them might turn up!

The second bean is the storyteller. When I was young and didn't know any better, I et a story bean, and it grew into a bean tree inside my head. Every bean on it has a story inside. Lots of them are about Jack and the things he done when he was off adventurin'. A dried-up old bean may not look too interesting by itself, but when it's planted in fertile soil and sleeps in the dark and wet for a while, it grows into a young green thing—eager to start all over again.

The third bean is you—a young-un who could do either thing. You could get the beans, plant them, and *find* the way to an adventure, or swallow them and let the adventure grow inside yourself. It's even possible for you to do both. Life lets everyone live lots of stories—each in its good time.

Right now you're asking to hear the old stories that keep coming young. That's the way it should be, for stories are a little like maps. They show us where someone found treasure and where there was danger. They point the way to mountains and warn us of the cliffs. They tell us where the lakes and oceans are, so we can decide whether to walk along the banks or cross over and whether we'll need a boat or we'll swim across.

The funny thing about maps is this: If you know where you want to go, they'll help you get there. But if you have no idea where you want to go, they may plant the idea in your head of an adventure you might never have thought of otherwise. And then it's very handy to know where the road twists and turns.

It may be that your road will take you where you will *need* help. And if you've been nice to fellow travelers, Old Graybeard may give you the magic to fly or breathe underwater. Right now you need the answers to your questions— some stories to help you grow. All you have to do is ask, set still, and listen. The stories are waiting for you, just like you're waiting for them.

So all three of us "human beans" are important: the hero, the storyteller, and the listener. They go around and around. The listener may become the doer. The doer may become the storyteller. The storyteller may become young again. The hero may pause to remember when he was a listener or pay particular attention so that he can become a teller later on.

Whenever I hear folks talking about their family tree, or the tree of life, I just naturally think about the bean tree. Whether we're part of the roots or one of the little bitty branches, just getting started, we're all connected. We're all part of the tree of life.

You're in luck this evening, because I've got some good stories in my head that are just right for the telling.

Jack and the
Northwest Wind

ne winter it got so cold it seemed like nobody could live through it. Jack and his maw was living alone in their rickety old cabin. Jack's paw and brothers were off working somewhere; there was hardly any food, and the Northwest Wind would come up at night and blow long and loud.

"*Whoooooo, whoooo, whooo* are these puny little humans clinging on to the side of the mountain? *Wheee, wheee, wheee,* I'll just blow them clean awayyyyy." He'd already blown off part of the shingles and most of the chinking from between the logs. Then the wind blew right on through, carrying away cornmeal, taters, socks, or anything else that was lying around loose. Jack wanted to fix the chinking, but the ground was too hard to dig any clay. There were no planks in the woodshed to nail over the openings. It started to look as if Jack and his maw might freeze to death.

But Jack, being an enterprising little feller, decided to do something about the state of affairs.

"I'm just going to go up there and find the hole the wind comes through and stuff my old hat in it," he told his maw.

"Oh, Jack, ye'd never make it that far," his maw moaned. "Nobody has ever been to the Northwest Wind."

"Well, I'd just as soon freeze on the way as freeze here," said Jack. His maw saw there wasn't no use in arguing with him, so she made him a pone to take along. Then he chopped her enough wood to see her through while he was away.

Jack set off with the first light of day, going straight to the northwest. He had to lean right into the wind and hold his hat on, while his ragged old coat just flapped around him.

"Hoooo, hooooo, heeee, HEEEEEEE." The wind seemed to be laughing at him.

He struggled on till he came to an old man standing by the road, chopping wood. "Howdy, Jack, where ye going this cold winter day?"

"I'm going to stop the Northwest Wind from blowing," Jack told him.

"Why, Jack, no one can stop the wind from blowing till the spring comes, and it's deep wintertime now."

"Sure I can," said Jack. "Just as soon as I find the hole the wind is blowing out of."

*He struggled on till he came to an old man standing
by the road, chopping wood.*

"That's a long way, Jack. Help me carry a load of wood home, and I'll feed ye up a bit 'fore ye go on."

So Jack helped the old man home with his wood and warmed himself up at the wood stove. The old man pulled a tablecloth out of the cupboard and laid it out on the table. Then he stood back and shouted in a loud voice:

"Spread, tablecloth! Spread!"

In an instant the tablecloth was covered with all the good things Jack could imagine—things he'd dreamed about but never eaten.

"Now, Jack," said the old man, "be a reasonable feller. It's another day's journey to the house of the Northwest Wind. If you freeze or get et up by polar bears, who's going to look after your maw then?"

Jack just hung his head.

"I've got plenty of provisions for the winter. You take this tablecloth and go back home to your maw tonight. She's probably worried sick about you," the old man reasoned.

It didn't take too much convincing to get Jack to agree, so the old man gave him the cloth. "Now don't you stop anywhere along the way, Jack. There're lots of dishonest people between here and home."

On the way back home Jack saw some boys playing on the ice, and they wheedled and called him to stop and play with them for a while. There didn't seem to be no harm in it, so Jack stopped and played awhile. The boys got to pestering him about the tablecloth over his arm, and finally he admitted that it was magic.

"Lord, Paw would love to see that!" the boys said. "Come on back and spend the night with us and show it to him." It was getting on toward dark, so Jack went back to their house for the night.

Their paw came home when it was near dark, and since they didn't have no maw and seemed to have no vittles, Jack put the tablecloth on their old splintery table and said in a loud voice:

"Spread, tablecloth! Spread!"

The cloth spread itself with venison haunches and roast pigs, and bottles of wine, and candied sweet potatoes, and everything else them people was wishing for.

Well, you never saw such a sight as what happened next. Them boys and their paw flew in on that table and started stuffing food in their mouths with their hands—didn't even bother with knives and forks. They leaned all over the table and drooled food every which way and belched and grabbed and stuffed like a bunch of hogs at a trough. Jack didn't know what to make of it. It made him think again about the good manners his maw had taught him. They made such a mess out of the table that Jack lost his appetite just looking at them. After they'd eaten all they could hold, Jack shook out the tablecloth and folded it up. He reckoned he was lucky they hadn't et it, too.

Now you-uns recollect how the old man had warned Jack about some dishonest folks 'round those parts. It's a shame he didn't remember, 'cause he'd done come to the very house where they lived. While Jack was sleeping, they slipped in and changed the magic cloth for an ordinary one that looked so much like it that Jack never noticed the difference when he started out in the morning.

When he got home, his maw was glad to see him. She said, "I guess you didn't make it. That old wind is still a-blowin'."

"No, Maw, but I got us something wonderful. This here cloth is magic. It will cover itself with food whenever I say the word."

"I sure would like to see that," said his maw.

Jack spread the cloth on the table, but no matter how many times he shouted, "Spread, tablecloth! Spread!" nothing at all happened.

"Well, Jack," said his maw, "that tablecloth ain't worth doodly-squat, seein' as how we've got no *food* to eat *anyway*. I might just as well cut it up and make ye a shirt out of it."

When Jack woke up the next day, the wind was blowing harder than ever, so he determined to try again. He cut his maw another mess of firewood and started out.

He was ashamed to see the old man again after what had happened, so he cut through a field and went a different way. He came to a mill grinding corn, and the miller stepped out.

"Howdy, Jack, are ye back so soon?" Bedad, it was the same old man that give Jack the tablecloth. He invited Jack in to get warm and have some of the food he had cooking on the stove. Jack told him all that had happened and how the tablecloth wouldn't work when he got it back home.

"Well, Jack, it's no wonder. Them folks are a bad lot. I reckon they done pulled the old switcheroo on ye. Didn't ye remember that I told you not to stop anywhere?"

Jack had to admit that he plumb forgot the warning.

"Now lookee here, boy. You're just going to freeze to death if you try to get to the Northwest Wind's place. Let me help ye out again. This here chicken is magic. You just set her on the table like this, and say:

"Come, gold! Come!

"And she'll lay ye a golden egg quick as that!"

Sure enough, at the old man's words, the chicken laid a perfect golden egg.

So Jack agreed to return to his maw with the chicken. Then the old man warned him again not to stop anywhere on the way. But it seems like that boy couldn't never remember what he wasn't supposed to do till he'd already done it. I've knowed lots of boys like that.

When he got to the place where the bad boys lived, they were just building a snowman, and they begged Jack to come on and join them. It looked like so much fun that he just couldn't resist. By the time they were finished they'd nagged at Jack till he admitted that the chicken was magic.

"Lord, Paw would sure like to see that, Jack. Stay the night and show it to him," they nagged. So he went back into their raggedy old house. Course, Jack didn't see hide nor hair of his tablecloth neither. Them boys were too smart for that!

Jack showed them how the chicken could lay golden eggs, and in the night, sure enough, while Jack slept, they changed chickens on him. And he pulled out for home with an ordinary old hen.

Just like before, the hen wouldn't lay gold for his maw, and she didn't half believe his story. She put him to bed, killed the chicken, and made up a fine pot of chicken and dumplings.

The wind blew for two more days worse than ever. It blew snow through the cracks and blew down the chimney so hard and long that it might nigh put out the fire. Jack was good and mad this time. "I'm going to stop that wind for sure this time, or I'm not coming back at all," he said.

"Well, what'll that prove, Jack?" asked his maw, but she knowed she couldn't change his mind once he had it set on something. He chopped his maw some more firewood and set off early in the morning.

He sure didn't want to see the old man this time, so he cut through the woods. But right in the thickest part he come upon the old man, out rabbit hunting.

"Lord, Jack, are ye up here again so soon?" the old man asked.

Jack had to admit that on the way home he had stopped at the boys' house again. The chicken he took home hadn't laid any golden eggs, and his maw was beginning to think he was right tetched in the head.

"Well, of course, Jack, them boys and their paw switched chickens on ye. I warned ye, didn't I? Well, never mind. Come on back to my house. I have something that'll help ye out."

"But I have to go stop the wind so Maw and I don't freeze. We can't hardly keep the fire going well enough to keep us warm."

"There's no way for ye to get there in this blizzard," the old man said.

Jack went home with the old man and got warm and fed, and the old man give him a knotty-looking little cudgel.

"This cudgel will beat apart anything you set it on. Come on outside and I'll show you. See that big old log there? All I have to say is:

"Play away, club! Play away!
Knock me some firewood!"

No sooner were the words out of the man's mouth than the club flew through the air and knocked that log into small pieces of firewood, just the right size for the fireplace. Jack had never seen anything like it.

"Jack, you go on home now. Forget about the Northwest Wind. Take this club, and remember that it will beat anything you like, for as long as you like."

Jack started back home again with his club over his shoulder. He didn't even go near the house where them rowdy boys lived, but who should he meet on the road but that very bunch, coming back from the store with big sacks?

"Howdy, Jack, where ye bound for this time?" they teased him.

"I'm on my way home, and I don't have time for you lot."

"Oh, come on, Jack, can't ye even be neighborly? What are ye feared of?" They kind of dared him like, you see.

Jack's hackles rose up like they expected. "I ain't afeard of nothing or nobody! And besides, this here cudgel is magic and will beat anything for as long as I want it to." Then Jack showed them how the cudgel worked.

"Well," they said, "come over to the house and set apiece."

Jack couldn't abide being put down by nobody, so he went with them and set there while they unloaded all the store-bought goodies they'd got with the golden eggs from *his* chicken. Try as he might, he couldn't keep his eyes open, and he fell asleep right in his chair.

The boys' paw come in, and they told him about Jack's magic cudgel.

"It's too dark to see outside," their paw said. "See if it'll work on that big log over there by the fireplace."

One of the boys slipped the cudgel out of Jack's hand and whispered:

"Play away, club! Play away!
Beat that log into kindling."

Sure enough, the cudgel lit into that log and began to beat it into kindling. But the noise woke Jack up. He saw right away what was happening, and he shouted:

"Play away, club! Play away!
Beat this house into sticks.
And beat these people
Till they give me back
My tablecloth and chicken."

The cudgel knocked in a wall and was starting in on the fireplace when they all hollered, "Stop, stop, we'll give them back."

Then Jack made them promise that they'd never rob any more travelers along that road. He took his tablecloth, chicken, and cudgel back to his own home.

His maw was glad to see that they had enough food and firewood to get them through the winter. The golden eggs even gave them enough money to hire some hands to fix up the house.

Jack never did get to see the place where the Northwest Wind come out, but like the old man suggested to him, it's not a good thing for folks to go messing 'round with the natural seasons.

He and his maw made out fine anyway.

The Lion
and the Unicorn

ere's a story about Jack when he was about half-growed. His maw sent him to the settlement to buy some store-bought goods like lye, salt, and pepper. She packed him some food to take along.

It was a right long way to town, so Jack picked up a piece of poplar wood and started to whittle as he walked. Like most days, he was wishing something grand and adventuresome would happen to him. And you know how it is; you've got to be careful what you wish for, 'cause you just might get it!

Jack wasn't paying much attention to what he was whittlin'. First thing he knowed, he'd made a paddle like his maw used for scooping butter from her churn. He bored a hole in the handle, tied a piece of string through it, and swung it 'round as he ambled on. Soon he come to a mudhole by the side of the road where bluebottle flies was sucking up water. He swung his paddle at them—*whack!* And seven of them fell over dead. Then he went down the road singing to himself:

> *"Big man Jack*
> *Killed seven at a whack.*
> *Seven at a whack*
> *For strong man Jack."*

Around lunchtime he met a man with a pack on his back, an old slouch hat on his head, and some kind of outlandish coat covered with patches and sich.

"Howdy, stranger," said Jack.

"No stranger than you," said the man. "Where ye off to?"

"Goin' to the settlement," said Jack. "And you?"

"Traveling over the world, blacksmithing, fixing harnesses, and looking for odd jobs," said the man.

Jack was mighty eager to know what it was like out in the world. So he asked the man, "Whyn't ye set here with me for a spell and have some lunch?"

"Thankee, lad," said the man. "I could do with a bite of something."

Jack opened his lunch. There was two of everything—food for going *and* coming. There were cold biscuits, ham, a fresh mater to slice, and a pair of his maw's fried apple pies.

After they was done, the stranger said, "That was fine eatin', son. Can I do anything to repay your kindness?"

"Have ye got airy studs in that pack of yourn?"

"Plenty to spare."

"Well," said Jack, "could you write on my belt 'Killed Seven at a Whack'?"

The man kind of grinned. "Hand it over." And in no time, he had put those words on Jack's belt in shiny letters.

"You must be going to see King Botchfit," said the feller.

"I might, and I might not. Why do ye ask?"

"Well, I heard tell the king was looking for a strong man to do a job of work. If you killed seven at a whack, you might just fit the bill."

Jack turned his footsteps toward the town. He was thinking all the way about the king's job and how it sounded mighty like an adventure. He bought his maw's provisions and asked the storekeeper if he knew where the king's house was.

"Sure, you can't miss it," the man answered. "It's the big white house on the hill with all the flags flying."

Jack knowed he ought to go on home, but he thought it wouldn't hurt if he was to just go up and find out what the king's job might be. When he got there, he saw lots of wagons and horses around the king's house, and his men were everywhere. They was riding and playing cards and doing odd chores.

"I wonder why he needs another man with so many

around already?" Jack asked himself. But he went to the door anyway and asked to see King Botchfit.

The king kind of sniggered when he saw Jack, but then he caught sight of Jack's belt. "Are those words on your belt true?"

"Yes, sir, true as they can be." Jack grinned.

"Well, ye don't look like much. But I've got a hundred men, and ain't one of them can kill seven men with one whack. Whyn't ye come in, and I'll tell ye what I need done." He took Jack in and give him some lemonade and cookies.

"We got us a wild boar and a unicorn raging around the countryside—tearing up crops, driving off livestock, and scaring folks half to death. I'd give ye five hundred dollars each to get rid of them. My men have tried, but they've gommed it up every time."

Well, what could Jack say? He'd only killed seven bottle flies, and the king was thinking it was seven men. He couldn't tell the truth now, with all them grown men looking at him.

"Sure, King Botchfit, I'd be glad to help ye out. I'll just come back tomorrow bright and early."

"Shucks, Jack, whyn't ye start out and get the old boar right now? You could be back here before dinnertime."

"That'll be fine," said Jack. "Which way do I go?"

"My men'll show you where he hangs out. Why don't ye leave your poke here? It'll be safe." The king was pretty smart in some ways.

Then he gave Jack a horse and gun and sent three men

along with him. They rode up in the woods about a half hour, and then the men showed Jack the place where the boar was seen the day before.

Soon as Jack was off his horse, they took off tail over nose!

"If they're in such a hurry to get away, that boar must be some kind of critter," said Jack. "I'd better get my skinny self out of here!" He set off in the direction he thought must be home. But he hadn't gone three steps when he heard a snortin' and a thumpin' comin' his way. "Tarnation!" he thought. "I'm in for it now!"

Just then he caught sight of the boar. It wasn't running *through* the bushes; it was tromping *over* 'em. That boar was coming at Jack with its red eyes blazing and its pestle tail up over its back like a banner.

Jack didn't wait for a second look. He took his foot in his hand and lit out through the woods. He zigged this way and zagged thataway, with that boar a-gainin' on him. His breath was about give out, when he saw an old corncrib up ahead. He ran and jumped up on it, but the boar was so close that it bit a piece out of his shirttail as he climbed up.

The roof of the crib was mostly rotted away, and Jack could see the critter walking 'round and looking in at the door. It decided it could get at him through the corncrib, so it come in and rared up, trying to get at him. It was gnashing its tushes and squealing, and its breath nearly knocked Jack over.

Jack waited till the boar was in midjump. Then he

hopped down, ran around, slammed the door, and wedged it shut 'fore that old boar knew what was goin' on. Boars is evil-tempered, but they ain't knowed for their brains.

When Jack seen it couldn't get out, he went on back to the king's house. By the time he got there, he'd forgot about being so scared. He was even swaggering a little.

"I never thought to see ye back . . . so soon," said the king. "Couldn't ye find him, Jack?"

"Naw, I looked everywhere for him," said Jack. "But I couldn't find nothing but a little piney woods rooter. I played with him awhile, but he got nasty and bit a chunk out of my shirt, so I flung him in an old corncrib up yonder in the woods. We can go back and see if that's what ye're after."

So Jack, the king, and a dozen men went back to the corncrib. By now that boar was ragin' to get out. There wasn't one of the king's men brave enough to go near it.

"We've got to kill it," said the king. "It's like to get out of there any minute!"

"Give me your gun then," said Jack. He climbed up the outside of the corncrib and shot the boar right between the eyes.

The king's men skinned and dressed it, and they say it made a whole wagonload of meat. The king give Jack his five hundred dollars, and they had supper together. Jack went to bed early. He was plumb wore-out from the day.

'Round about daylight the king come and got him out of bed. "Jack, ye got to get up quick! That unicorn has been rousting about the town overnight. I want ye to go after it quick as ye can."

"King," said Jack, pulling on his trousers, "I ain't never hunted no unicorn, nor nothin' else, before I had my breakfast."

There was nothing for it. Jack got washed up and had breakfast with the king while he heard stories about the carousing that unicorn done overnight.

When he'd stalled as long as he could, Jack went with the king's men out to an orchard. Apples, branches, and twisted-off trees were everywhere. The king's men disappeared even quicker this time.

"If that critter can do this kind of damage, there's no way I'm going to stay here and wait for it," said Jack. "I'm five hundred dollars ahead now. I can go home and have a good time. If I stay here and get killed, there ain't no amount of money can make up for it."

So he started home again. But he hadn't got much past the edge of the orchard when he heard the unicorn a-coming. It was moving so fast it sounded like a big wind blowing up. The rumble of its hooves was like summer thunder. There was no place to go, so Jack stood his ground.

Up come the unicorn bucking and prancing, with the sun on its horn and its white coat so bright that Jack's eyes hurt to look at it. Scared as he was, it was a wonder to behold that unicorn.

"Well, lightning horse, I never saw the beat of you," said Jack.

The unicorn whinnied like it was laughing. It gave one flick of its mane, pawed the earth, and then it come on sizen at Jack. It swung its sharp horn from side to side like a man cutting wheat.

Flick! Flack! Then it got the bead on Jack and charged at him with its horn lowered. Jack saw which way it was coming and jumped out of the way at the last minute.

Whooosh, the wind of its passing nearly knocked Jack over. Again it charged. Again he jumped out of its way. But Jack was studying the unicorn all the while, and he saw that its eyes were on the sides of its head, like a cow or deer. Besides that, it had that big twisty horn right in the middle of its forehead. Once it lowered its head and started running, it couldn't see where it was going.

Jack had dodged many a bull, and he was wise in the way of critters. Next time the unicorn come sizen at him, he stood right smack-dab in front of a giant oak tree. As soon as it lowered its head and charged, Jack stepped aside.

Whooosh! ZZZZZapppp! The unicorn's twisty horn went plumb through that oak tree and out the other side. Jack had some nails in his pocket, and he wedged the horn in even tighter.

The unicorn pulled and twisted and cried, but there was no way for it to get free. So Jack stuck his hands in his pockets and went a-whistlin' down to the king's house.

"Ye're back mighty quick, Jack," said the king. "Didn't ye have no luck?"

"I'm back for lunch. The only thing I saw out there was a

little cow with only one horn. I played with it, but it got too rough. I got mad and picked it up by its hind leg and its ear and stove its horn into a tree. We can go look at it if ye want to."

The king couldn't wait till lunch—he was that excited! He took Jack and a passel of his men straight back to where Jack had left the unicorn, which was plumb tuckered out by the time they got there. It stood there shining blue lightning bolts out of its eyes.

"Pretty little thing, ain't it?" said Jack.

"Jack, I tell ye the truth," said the king. "I ain't never seen a finer specimen, and hit alive, too. Most times ye got to shoot 'em. I hear tell there's a zoo somewhere up north looking for one. I'll write this afternoon and tell them we got a beastie for 'em."

Jack liked that idea fine. The king gave him his five hundred dollars and showed him a shortcut back home.

He wasn't hardly out of sight, though, when a messenger come riding up to the king's house in a real sweat. "Quick, King, ye got to do something! There's a wild lion loose in the village, raging around and doing all kinds of damage. They say it come over from Tennessee!"

"I'll swan," said the king. "I wish you'd come sooner! I just let the only man go that can handle this job. Maybe I can catch him."

The king knew which way Jack went, so he jumped on his horse and lit out after him. It didn't take long before he saw Jack up ahead.

"Hey there, Jack, wait up. I've got another job of work for ye."

When Jack heard the king's voice behind him, he kind of hunched up his shoulders and walked on like he didn't hear him. But it wasn't no use. The king was determined to get Jack back.

He rode his horse up to Jack. "Come back," said the king. "There's a wild lion loose in the town. You got to come back and catch him for me."

"I'd like to help ye, King, but I'm already late for another appointment. I've got to get home today. Besides"—he sneaked a look up at the king's face—"I'd be losing money if I came back to your place."

"Blame it, Jack, money is no problem," the king insisted. "Why, I'd give ye a thousand dollars to get shet of that lion."

"Well," said Jack, "I guess I could come back and give ye a hand just for a little while."

"Oh, Jack, I'd be much obliged. Here, jump up on my horse and we'll save some time."

But by the time Jack and the king got back to town, the lion had already stolen a sheep and headed for the hills. Jack set off in the direction it had gone.

Soon as he was out of sight of the king, though, Jack started to thinking. "Here I am with a thousand dollars in my pocket. My maw is going to skin me for being away so long, and I'm off on some fool errand—lion chasing! I think I'll just sneak off home."

Jack didn't know it, but the lion had just caught his scent and was heading after him. This particular lion always did prefer boy to sheep.

Jack heard it coming. *Paddity paddity, walkie, stalkie. Crash, bash, gnash.* It was like a giant tomcat after its prey, only a hundred times bigger.

Jack shinnied up a tree, just in time to hear the lion's jaws go *clack* right at his heels. He climbed as high as he could go, then looked back down. Sitting under the tree was the biggest kitty Jack had ever seen. It had a right pretty face, but its fangs were as long as Jack's fingers, and its mane was big as a washtub.

It stretched up and sharpened its claws on the tree trunk, licking its chops and smiling at Jack. There were scars all over its nose from times when it had fought wars and won.

"If I get kilt today," moaned Jack, "it serves me right for bein' stupid enough to get into this mess. That lion just et a sheep. It ain't goin' to get hungry and go away anytime soon."

The lion frisked around the tree, trying to entice Jack down to play. Then it got tired of waiting and began to chew on the tree, trying to chew it down. But it was a very big tree, and the lion was very full of sheep. Finally it yawned and went to sleep under the tree so Jack couldn't sneak away.

But when Jack heard it snoring, he decided that was the only chance he had. So he started down, reeeal slow and careful. But as bad luck would have it, he put his foot down on a brickle limb.

The limb broke under his weight, and down he come — *caterwampus*—on that lion's back. Well, that lion took off roarin' like all the devils in hell was after it. Jack managed to get right ways on its back and held on to its mane for dear life.

The lion run down to the courthouse square, 'round and 'round. The king was there on business. And his men started trying to get a bead on the lion without shooting Jack or some innocent bystander.

Finally one of them shot the lion dead, and Jack fell off into the mud. Just about then the king come out and saw what had happened.

Jack went up to the king, mad as a hornet. "Now lookee here what your men done!"

"Looks to me like they saved your life, Jack," said King Botchfit.

"No, sir, that's not even close to what happened!" shouted Jack. "I was training that lion to be a ridy-horse fer ye. Wouldn't you have looked grand riding around on your own trained pet lion? Now your men have done killed it."

"Lordy," said the king, studying the big dead lion. "You men have done spoiled it all. You've got to raise another five hundred dollars to pay Jack for his work. Why, you could have kilt *him!*"

Jack went back to the king's house, had a bath, and got a new suit of clothes, because his had got spoilt in the mud. The king give him a thousand dollars, and the king's men give him another five hundred. He stayed one more night with the king, having dinner and swapping stories.

The limb broke under his weight, and down he come —
caterwampus — on that lion's back.

Next morning Jack finally got started for home, with his poke full of store-bought goods. The only thing he had to worry about was what his maw was going to say to him for being three days late. But he reckoned as how all that money he had was going to make Maw settle down right quick.

The Longest
Story

ne time the king put out the word that he would give his daughter and half of everything he owned to the man who could tell the longest story. The king would set up his two-hour glass, and any man whose story stopped before the sand run through it would have to come and join the king's army.

Well, a lot of men tried it, and a lot of men failed. The king's army got to be might nigh the biggest in all these mountains. Couldn't nobody come up against him.

After a while Jack heard about the king's offer and reckoned he'd try it; he was a good un for telling long

He took along his whittlin' knife.

stories. He took along his whittlin' knife and set down to tell his tale. And this was it:

"One time there was a king who decided to gather enough grain in his warehouse to feed his people for three winters. The people all brought in their corn and wheat and stored it. But there was one little bitty hole in the northwest corner, and a little field mouse got in, and it carried away one kernel of corn.

"It took this corn back to its nest and then came back for another one. It took this corn to its nest and then came back after another one. It took this grain of corn back to its nest and then came back after another one. . . ."

And on he went and on till the king was might nigh falling asleep.

"Ain't ye never going to tell me what happened next?" asked the king.

"Sure," said Jack, "but it'll probably take him a week just to empty the warehouse."

The king could see he was outsmarted. "Blame it all, take my daughter!" he shouted.

So Jack did.

Jack and Catherine

ack and his brothers, Tom and Will, didn't get on too well. Jack was the youngest and kinda like his mother's pet. The older boys was jealous of Jack. Sometimes they done real mean things to him to get even 'cause they thought he had it too soft.

Their paw had decided it was time for the three of them to go out in the world and try their luck. He give them each twenty dollars (which was a heap of money in those days) and told them to come back in a year and see who'd done the best.

Tom and Will went into town and bought themselves good suits of clothes fit for adventuring. But Jack didn't want to spend his money on clothes. He thought there might be something more important down the road.

Tom and Will didn't want to let Jack come with them. "You're too ragged and dirty to be seen with. We'll never get a job of work with you tagging along," they said. But Jack insisted, and there was no help for it.

They all set out together with Maw just a-weeping behind her apron and Paw leaning on his hoe, waving them on. What the parents didn't know was that Tom and Will had laid a plan to do Jack out of his money. They didn't let on till they was well away from that part of the country where anybody knowed them. It happened when they come to a crossroad where two branches of the road split off in different directions.

Tom and Will lit into Jack and beat him up. They split his money and threw him in a swamp for dead. "Good riddance to that nuisance of a boy," they said. "No one will ever know what happened to him."

Then Tom took the left fork, and Will took the right, going off to seek their fortunes with their new clothes and Jack's money.

But the mud in that swamp healed Jack up and brought him back to life. Jack come to, bruised and feeling mad, and he thought about what he should do next. He wasn't too far from home; he could have gone back. But Jack weren't no tattletale, and he decided to go on even without any money.

He threw his hat in the air to see which road he should take, and it landed in the middle, so he went on straight ahead. He traveled on, traveled on, with the road getting narrower and more overgrown till it wasn't much more than a path. Bats was flying overhead and owls had started their moaning when Jack caught sight of a house off to the side. It was almost covered over with briers and vines, but he could see it was a fine big house. He was so ragged and dirty that he hated to call out, but he was tired and needed a place to spend the night, so he went on up. The only living soul he saw was a big calico cat. She was chasing her tail around and around, widdershins, widdershins, widdershins.

Jack called out, "Hallooo, anybody home?"

"Just the cat and mouse," said the cat, looking at him right solemn.

"Ay, law," said Jack, "I've done come to a country where cats can talk."

"Well, I haven't always been a cat," the cat said. "There's a horrible old witch around these parts. She got my whole family. This here little mouse is my sister. The witch turned her into a cat and then a mouse. She's coming back in three days to do the same to me."

"That's not right," said Jack. "What can I do to help ye?"

"It's too late for my sister," said the cat, "but you could help me turn back if ye start tonight."

The cat and mouse showed Jack where there was some food and told Jack what he must do.

"Tonight the witch is going to send all sorts of big animals—bears, pant'ers, and sich. You'll have to fight them and keep them from coming in. If ye can do that, we'll all be safe for one more night."

Jack found a big old cudgel by the woodshed and waited

by the door. He was tired and sore from the bruises his brothers give him, but Jack was the kind of feller could get a new wind when he had to. And that was a good thing, because soon as the dark of the moon had fallen, fierce critters came at him from all sides. There were bears and alligators and pant'ers and Jack couldn't see what else. They all had shiny teeth and eyes, and they all growled and roared and spit.

Somehow Jack got through the night, but when the light come up, there wasn't hide nor hair of any of the beasts he'd fought during the night. The little calico cat come out, but she was bigger now and had started to look a little like a girl.

"You did it, Jack. I knew ye could. But now come on in and get some food and rest. Tonight the witch will send middle-size animals, and you have to fight them off, too."

Sure enough, with the black night, a new attack began. This time there were bobcats, weasels, polecats, badgers, and who knows what other demon animals. Jack fought and clubbed and beat them off again.

This time when the cat came out, Jack could see that she really was a girl, but she still had whiskers and claws and pretty pointed ears like a cat.

"Tonight, Jack, you'll have to fight little critters. But some of them is pizen, and some of them can sting ye to death, so you'd best be ready," the cat girl warned him.

Jack carved himself some paddles and swats so he'd be ready for this lot, too. Well, you wouldn't have known how many little fierce things there were till that night on the cat

*This time when the cat came out, Jack could see
that she really was a girl.*

girl's porch. Jack had to fight off pizen snakes, spiders, and scorpions, vampire bats, and every kind of hornet on this Earth. There was even centipedes big as Jack's shoe that turned up 'specially for the occasion.

Jack fought and stamped and swatted and smacked all night. And by the time the sun come up, he didn't have a dab of energy left. Well, not until the door opened, anyhow. There stood the prettiest redheaded girl Jack had seen in all his life.

"Ye done well, Jack. Now I'm Catherine again, instead of a cat. Come on in, and I'll fix you some food. Tonight there's only the old witch herself to deal with. The one thing you have to remember is not to let her do anything for ye. She'll try, but if you let her, she'll change you and me both into cats, and there'll be no one to save us. We'll end up mice like my pore little sister."

Jack got some rest, and toward evening he got ready to meet the old witch. He settled down by the fire with a needle and thread and started to patch his old raggedy coat. Well, pretty soon there was a blowing and rumbling like a bad storm coming on. A big old wind blew the door open, *whoosh*, and in come that witch.

There's lots of witches in this world. There's pretty ones and homely ones, good ones and bad ones. But this one was the Witch of the World. Nobody was ever as ugly or mean as that old hag standing before Jack. She had the kind of face that could turn milk sour.

"Howdy, Jack, we meet at last," she said, stretching her old claws out toward the fire.

Jack's stomach turned over, but he didn't let on. "Howdy, ma'am."

"What in tarnation are ye doing there, boy, tying that jacket up in knots? Here, let me mend it for ye."

"I'll do my own mending, thankee," Jack told her, kind of stifflike.

He finished mending his jacket and put it back on. Then he set about making some corn pone.

"I can't stand to see a man messing around with food. It's so awkward. Let me do that for ye," said the witch.

"I'll fix my own pones," said Jack, and he finished mixing them and set them over the fire. Then he got a skillet and put some meat on to fry. Well, Jack turned around for a second, and the old witch picked up a fork and went to turn Jack's meat.

He caught sight of her out of the corner of his eye and flew at her to grab the fork. But he was moving so fast that he knocked her right into the fire.

Well, such a crackling, sparkling, and exploding you never saw in all your life. There was nothing left of that old witch except a nasty smell of sulfur in the air.

Catherine came out from her hiding place and give Jack a big hug. "Ye done it, Jack. We're shet of that old witch and her ways for good."

In the morning, when it was light, Catherine took Jack out and showed him 'round the farm. All the brambles and bushes had disappeared. The pasture was full of pretty horses, cows, chickens, and sheep. There were fields of growing crops and orchards full of fruit. There was even a strongbox filled with gold. Catherine's people had been rich farmers before the witch came along.

Jack looked around at all he saw, and his heart kind of sank. "I'd been thinking I'd like to marry you, but I'm just a pore boy, and you have all this land and livestock and money."

Catherine threw back her head and laughed. "You saved it all from the witch, and my life, too. You're the bravest man I ever met. Our gettin' married is a wonderful idea."

So they hooked the surrey up to a pair of fine horses and went off to town. They bought Jack a fine suit and found a preacher to marry them. Then they went back home to mind their farm.

Jack and Catherine was good helpmates to each other. She could cook and sew; Jack knew how to plow and plant and reap and sow. And they had plenty of money for whatever they wanted.

But Jack was watching the calendar. He knew that the year was almost up, and the day was coming for him to return home. He hitched up the surrey and put his old ragged clothes under the seat. Then he set off with Catherine for his homeplace. They got to the fork in the road, and Jack told Catherine what had happened there. She was pretty mad at his brothers, but Jack made her promise not to tell airy soul.

When they got to the last bend in the road, Jack stopped the wagon and put his old clothes back on. He messed up his hair and rubbed some dirt on his face. "Wait here for me. I'll just go and see what's happened while I've been gone."

Jack's paw saw him coming and was right glad. "Law, Jack, looks like you didn't do too well out in the world. Let me run get you some of my clothes so you don't look so raggedy."

"No, Paw, I reckon I'll just go as I am."

His maw was glad to see him and hugged his neck. His brothers looked at him kind of sheepish, like they was wondering if he was going to tell on them. But they couldn't help being a little smart-alecky with him, 'cause they had good clothes and pretty wives. Folks that do you wrong are like that sometimes. Jack visited with them for a while and then said, "I left some things at my camp up in the woods. I'll be back directly."

Jack ran back to where Catherine was and washed his face in the stream. Then he put on his fine suit and hat, and they drove cloppity-clop right up to Jack's house, with all their fine harness shining and jingling.

His paw heard them coming and looked out. "Now who can that be, do you reckon?"

"Must be somebody rich; no one around here has a buggy like that," said Tom.

Jack's maw looked out. "Well, I declare, that's Jack. But who's that beautiful girl in the fine dress and bonnet? Why, she's even got a parasol."

Tom told his wife to hide under the bed. Will said to hisn, "Go hide yourself in the attic. You can't let them see you in that old cotton dress."

So Tom's wife hid under the bed, and Will's wife went and crawled up in the attic.

Jack and Catherine came in, and Jack introduced her. They talked for a little bit, and Catherine looked around.

"Tom and Will," she said, "Jack told me you two had wives, but I don't see them; aren't you going to introduce us?"

There was nothing to do but call out their wives. Both girls was covered with dust and feathers and spiderwebs and looked a sight worse than before.

"You men ought to be ashamed," Catherine told Tom and Will. "You just don't know how to treat a lady." The girls could tell they were going to like Catherine right off.

They had a big party that night with some of Maw's good fried chicken, mashed potatoes, turnip greens, and pumpkin pie. All of the boys talked about their adventures, but there was no question about who'd done the best.

The next day Jack took Paw and Maw back to his big farmhouse, and they all lived happy. Far as I know, Tom and Will never did amount to much.

Jack and
Uncle Thimblewit

ots of folks call Jack the Giant Killer. And he did kill right many of them. Giants belong to the old way, when there was plenty of room for them to move around without stepping on someone or kind of "accidentally" eating somebody's cows. I figure they must go back to the time of the dinosaurs, when everything on Earth was bigger. I've heard tell dinosaurs had an extra brain in their tails to help them get 'round curvy roads and tight places. Giants didn't come equipped that way.

But you know, Jack had a kind heart, and my favorite story was one my old Irish uncle used to tell. He was the one who always came to our house on foot once a year, with everything he owned tied up in a handkerchief hangin' off the end of this crooked stick. That and his stories was about all he had to call his own. We young-uns loved to see him comin', but my mommy didn't take to him and his gypsy ways.

She thought he was a bad influence on us just 'cause he kept one fingernail long for cutting the butter and sich things as that. We knew for sure we'd get a whupping if we done like him. My pappy said we should be good to him. A man that survived the potato famine was a good lesson in gratitude for us.

Well, the way he told the story, the king's son, Greatheart, was off seeking an adventure. He had with him plenty of money and two horses, because he was lookin' for a man who knew the country to guide him. He come to a town on the edge of the woods where there was all kinds of commotion going on. A heap of noisy people was gathered in the courthouse square. The sheriff and a judge was tryin' to keep order, and a plain wooden coffin was layin' there.

"What seems to be the trouble?" asked the king's son.

"This here gommer died with half his jobs unfinished and owing money to everyone in town," said the sheriff. "We're about to put him on trial for his unpaid debts."

"Well, I hate to see a man go unburied," said the prince. "Go and bury him decent. Tomorrow you can send everyone to me that has a debt against him, and I'll pay them all." Then he asked the way to the hotel and got a room for the night.

Now Jack happened to be in town, and he was out of a job.

So he went to Greatheart and offered to be his man. "I know this country like the back of my hand, and I can survive by my wits alone," Jack said. The prince hired Jack and put him up for the night.

The next morning there was a line outside the hotel where all the dead man's debtors was waiting for their money.

True to his word, Greatheart opened his purse and paid every penny that was owed. And by the time he was finished, his money was all gone except enough to pay for his room and Jack's and buy them both breakfast.

"Well, Jack, my friend, I'm afraid your job is off, for I've no money left to pay you."

"Never mind," said Jack. "That pore old dead man was a kind soul and a friend of mine. Money isn't everything; I'm glad to help ye out."

So they rode into the woods, merry enough for a while. But the woods was deep and dark and went on for miles. On top of that a storm come on, with thunder and lightning and buckets of rain. Toward nighttime they were tired, wet, and hungry. Greatheart was gettin' might low about his chances out in the world with no money to spend.

"Never fear," said Jack, "for my uncle Thimblewit lives near here. He's a giant, and he has plenty of everything. We can git our dinner there."

"I don't think that's a good plan, Jack," said Greatheart. "Thimblewit and my father are not exactly good friends. In fact, they've had a war on for as long as I can remember."

But Jack insisted, and by the time they got to the giant's

castle, Jack had a plan. "You wait here for me. I'll go on ahead."

Jack went up to the door, and beat on it as hard as he could with a stick. Finally Old Thimblewit come rumbling and stumbling to the door with his nightshirt on, for he'd already gone to bed.

"Who's bangin' on my door at this hour?" he shouted.

"It's me, your nephew Jack. I've got some dretful important news for ye."

"Well, Nephew, come in and welcome. Ain't seen ye for a coon's age."

Jack went in puffing like he was out of breath and looking over his shoulder. "Uncle, we got to hide ye, quick! The king's soldiers are coming."

"Nephew, I'm strong as an old hickory tree. I can lick five hundred of the king's men."

"Yes," said Jack, "but this time he's comin' with more'n a thousand."

At that Old Thimblewit went as pale as ashes. "At my age I can't handle that many. I'm afeard."

"Well, the way I figure it, Uncle, we'll just have time to get ye hid 'fore they come."

Thimblewit grabbed the cellar key with one hand, and Jack with the other, and run downstairs fast as he could go. "Here, Jack, lock me in the cellar. Come back and fetch me after the soldiers have gone."

"I will, Uncle. Now lay down here quiet as ye can. I'll tell them you've gone on a long trip."

*Finally Old Thimblewit come rumbling and stumbling
to the door with his nightshirt on.*

Jack went back upstairs and let Greatheart in. He told him what had happened. The two of them flung the furniture around and stamped up and down and made every kind of noise they could think of. They went downstairs and rattled the locked cellar door.

"Why is this door locked? Are you sure he's not in here?" shouted Greatheart.

"Oh, no," shouted Jack, "that's just a little broom closet; my uncle would never fit in there."

They tromped back upstairs, got warm and dry, and had them a good meal. Then they found the giant's money box and refilled the prince's purse. Jack took a couple of gold guineas himself. They had a good night's sleep, and in the morning Greatheart went down the road and hid.

Jack let Old Thimblewit out. "Thankee, Nephew," rumbled the giant. "You've saved my life. How can I ever repay you?"

"Lordy, Uncle, that's what kinfolks is for," said Jack. "But if I was you, I'd lay low for a while."

Jack went out and found Greatheart. The two of them rode off together and had some grand adventures, but those will have to wait till another time.

Jack and the Flying Ship

here was a king in some far-off county got into a fight with a witch, and the witch won. Just to prove that, she put a spell on his girl so she'd just sit and cry all the time and wouldn't comb her hair nor nothing. The king put out word that whoever could break the witch's spell could have half his kingdom and marry his daughter. The news finally reached this part of the mountains.

Since it was the old witch that put the spell on the girl, she was the one that would have to take it off. So the first thing was to find her and challenge her and make her let the girl go. So far lots of young men had tried and failed. Some of them were sons of rich men and kings.

But Will got it in his head that *he* could succeed. He was an arrogant sort of feller. Maw fixed him a road cake and got him a bottle of cider to take along. He packed his satchel and set out.

He traveled on, traveled on for miles, till he was footsore and hungry. Then he sat down by the road and took out his vittles. A pore old raggedy man with a long gray beard came draggin' down the road, leaning on a cane.

"Howdy, son," said the old man to Will. "I'm tired and hungry; could ye spare me something to eat?"

"Lordy, no, I've hardly got enough for myself," said Will, and he sat right there and ate every crumb. Then he went on, asking everyone which way it was to the witch's house.

He finally got there. She was out sweepin' the path. "Howdy, Will." She grinned at him. "I've been expectin' you."

"Then you know what I come for," he said.

"I do," she said, "but I don't think ye're man enough for all my contests. Ye'll have to beat me in every one."

"Try me, old lady," said Will.

"Don't say I didn't warn ye," she cackled. "Watch this!" She brought out a great old big hackle, like their maw used for combing sheep's wool. Only this one was at least a foot long. It was like something a giant might use. Then she got up on a stump, cut a double somersault in the air, come down on the hackle, and bounced off, good as new.

Well, Will thought if an old lady could do it, he could, too. So he got up on the stump, cut a somersault in the air, and landed on the hackle like the witch done, but he didn't bounce off. Those nails stove into his back and like near killed him.

Soon as he could move, he crawled off home. It took him several days. Everyone wanted to know what happened, but he turned his face to the wall and wouldn't talk to no one.

Tom was always trying to show Will up. He 'lowed as how he'd have a go. Maw fixed him up a cake and a bottle of cider, too, though it was just about all they had in the house. He set off early in the morning, just like Will, and sometime around afternoon he sat down to eat his dinner.

Sure enough, an old man come hobbling down the road to where Tom sat. He was all bent over and pitiful.

"Howdy, son!" he said. "I'm like to starve, would you spare some of your food?"

"Get away from here, you crazy old coot," said Tom. "I've hardly got enough for myself." And he stuffed every bit of that cake down his gullet.

"Then may you fare as well," said the old man, moving off down the road. Seemed as though he straightened up a little 'fore he was out of sight.

Tom got to the witch's house long before dark, and he was glad of that, because all kinds of night critters was already gathered there. Seemed like he could hear some snickering coming from under the house, though he couldn't see nothing, only some greeny eyes looking out at him.

"Howdy, Tom," the witch kind of snarled at him. He was some put out that she knowed his name, but he didn't let on.

"Howdy, Granny."

"I reckon ye've come for to free the king's gal?"

"Ye got it right, old woman."

"Well, young feller," she said, "whatever happens, remember you brought it on yourself."

She went and got her hackle and bounced off it like before. Then she bet Tom he couldn't do the same.

So Tom tried, and ended up crippled like Will. A few days later he dragged into home and fell into his bed, silent as a toad.

Jack got to pestering his maw about letting him go on the road, but after what happened to his big older brothers, she wasn't too happy about letting him go. Jack was just a slight feller. Besides that, she had nothing to send with him but an ash cake and a bottle of springwater. But there was no help for it. He nagged her till she let him go.

Jack set off whistling, and walked along, dreaming of what he'd find at the end of the road. In the afternoon he sat down in the shade to eat.

'Round the bend come that raggedy old man. "Howdy, son, could you spare some food for a hungry man?"

"Sure, Graybeard. It ain't much, but you're welcome to half of it."

The old man sat down on a rock and watched him. Well, Jack sure was surprised when he opened his poke. Instead of an ash cake, he found a big spice cake and a bottle of sweet wine. Him and Graybeard had them a fine lunch and sat swappin' stories for a while.

When the old man heard where Jack was going, he shook

his head. "That old witch, Mourning Belle, acts like she's got something stuck in her craw. She don't like no kind of man, and no one has beat her yet. Everyone who's tried has ended up crippled or dead."

"I ain't got much to lose," said Jack. "I reckon I'll give it a try."

"If you're determined to go, I might have something that will help you out," the old man told him. He rummaged around in his pockets, pulled out a little folded-up whimsy, and handed it to Jack.

"This is a ship, Jack. If you've got faith, you can take it over yonder in the grass and unfold it, and it'll get big enough to carry you and anybody else you meet."

Jack did like the old man said, and sure enough, that little bitty thing unfolded into a pretty sailing ship, just hoverin' over the top of the grass.

"This ain't no ordinary ship, Jack, for it can go on land *and* through the air. All you have to do is say:

"Sail, ship! Sail!

"It'll take you right to the witch's house if you tell it to. Just remember to stop and pick up anyone you see on the way. You'll need all the help you can get to outsmart that old woman. You'll need some money, too. There's a hundred dollars in this little sack. Pay me back when you have it."

Jack thanked the old man and set off in the little ship, sailing across the mountains and valleys, over treetops and fields. Jack looked down and saw a queer bald-headed feller below. He was running along, breaking up rocks and smashing trees with his head. Jack remembered what Graybeard had told him.

"Hallooo, Hardhead," Jack shouted to him, "would ye like to come aboard my ship?"

The bald feller looked up and nodded, so Jack put his ship down and took him aboard. "What's your name?" asked Jack.

"Hardy Hardhead," said the feller.

"Well, I got it half-right," said Jack.

They sailed on farther and saw a man in the field below, eating up cows as fast as he could catch them—horns, tails, hooves, and all.

"What's your name, stranger?" they called out to him.

"Eatwell's my name," he said.

"Would you like to try your fortune with us?" Jack asked.

The man nodded and ate up a whole cow while they were docking the ship. He clambered on board, and they sailed on.

Directly they saw a man with his mouth under a waterfall, drinking up all the water as it went over the cliffside.

"Hey, feller, whoever you are, want to come with us?" they called.

"I reckon so," said the feller. "My name's Drinkwell. Maybe I could find a decent drink somewhere out there in the world."

So they took him on and sailed until they saw someone

zoom past on the ground, leaving clouds of dust behind him. The funny thing about that was that he had one leg tied up behind his ear.

"You there, Speedwell," Jack called out to him, "looks like you belong with us." The feller nodded, ran up a mountain peak, and jumped right in the boat. They sailed on farther.

Down below they spotted a man with gigantic ears. He was standing with his left hand behind his ear, as if he were listening to something.

"Who are you?" called Jack and his crew.

"I'm Harkwell," said the man, "and I can hear a big ship grinding against an iceberg somewhere up north."

"Come aboard the ship. We may need you," called Jack.

Pretty soon they spotted someone standing on a mountain peak, looking off in the distance, shading his eyes.

"What are you looking at?" called Jack, circling the ship overhead.

"I'm looking at the lord mayor's parade over in England. That's why they call me Seewell."

"We could use you in our crew," said Jack. "We'll set down so you can come aboard."

They had hardly set sail when a bullet went zinging across their bow, and Jack looked down to see a man with his gun pointed almost straight up, the smoke just rising from the barrel.

"Listen, you trigger-happy booger," Jack called out, "you could have killed somebody."

"Naw," said the feller, "I missed you by a mile. I was shootin' the gun outa the hand of a stagecoach robber in Texas. See! I got him."

"Come along. I think we're going to need you, too, Shootwell."

So Shootwell came on the ship, and they headed for the witch's house.

They could see Mourning Belle out back of her house, burying something or someone. There were lots of patches of new-dug dirt nearby. When the shadow of Jack's ship fell across the grave, she looked up and waved.

Jack put the ship down and got out of it. Mourning Belle leaned the shovel up against the house like she might need it again real soon.

"Howdy, Jack." She grinned, kind of evil-like. "I reckon I know why ye're here."

"Yes'm," Jack answered. "Me and my men have come to ask ye to remove the spell from the king's daughter."

"Men, are they? Freaks more like! I hope for your sake that they're smarter than they look. I have four contests ye'll have to win. If ye lose any of them, I'll cut off your heads and bury you in my cornfield. It's a grisly crop I grow, my lad."

"We're not afeard of your contests, Mourning Belle," Jack said. "What's first?"

She looked at Jack right sharp. Witches never tell anyone their names; it takes away some of their power. She didn't let on that she was upset Jack knew her name, though. She just went to get her hackle like before.

She put the hackle by the stump, turned a double flip, and bounced off it like it was a bed.

"I've got a hundred dollars says there ain't no one in your crew can do that," she crowed.

Jack put down his hundred dollars and said, "Hardy Hardhead, can ye do it?"

Hardy Hardhead just nodded. Then he got up on the stump like the witch had done, cut a double flip, and landed on the hackle headfirst. *Screeech, creeech, crunch.* He knocked every tooth out of that hackle.

Mourning Belle rubbed her hands together and cackled. "Oh, goody, we get to go on. No one ever goes past that one."

Jack picked up his money. "What's next?" he asked.

"It's gettin' on toward dinnertime. I'll bet two hundred dollars ye ain't got anyone can outeat me."

"You're on," Jack laughed. "Eatwell can do it."

The old witch went out to the barn and came back with two fine steers. "When I give the signal, we both start eating. The first one to finish the whole beef wins."

Jack counted to three, and Mourning Belle and Eatwell started eating.

Eatwell finished his cow, a sheep, and a goat before the old girl had got started good.

"That was fine eatin'!" She seemed surprised. "But I'll bet four hundred dollars you can't win the next one."

Jack put down his hundred and the three hundred he'd won from the witch. "We're game," he said.

"This time," she told him, "you've got to get someone to outdrink me."

Drinkwell stepped up ready to go. "I've been dying of thirst all day."

Mourning Belle took him down to the cellar where she had her applejack stored. She set out six kegs of it for Drinkwell and six for herself. "Like before, we start on the signal. The first person to drink six kegs wins."

Jack counted to three, and the two of them started drinking. Drinkwell drank his six and three more while Mourning Belle was finishing up her first.

"Nick Slick! Stop!" she shouted. "I won't have enough to get me through the winter."

The witch drawed her eyes up to a slit and looked at Jack and his motley crew. "The way I figure it, son, y'all have just been lucky so far. Now we can get on to the most important contest."

"So far as I can reckon," said Jack, "this one ought to be worth about eight hundred dollars."

"Shucks," she said, "let's up it to a thousand. Have ye got that much?"

Well, Jack didn't, of course, but he decided to call her bluff.

"Listen here, Mourning Belle, it's time to stop messing around and go the whole hog. I'll bet my ship and all her crew. But iffen you lose, you've got to lift the spell from the princess, forever!"

Mourning Belle whistled, and her eyes got round as

"Nick Slick! Stop!" she shouted. "I won't have enough to get me through the winter."

saucers. She started off darin' Jack, and now he was darin' her. She couldn't rightly stand it. But she figured there wasn't any way she could lose, so she agreed. "That's a hard bargain, Jack, but I could use me a crew like you and your men. This contest is a race!"

Jack called up Speedwell.

"Here's the contest," said the witch. She got an egg from the henhouse, broke it open, and gave Speedwell half the shell.

"We're going to race to the ocean, eight hundred miles away, fill up this eggshell with seawater, and race back. The first one here with half an eggshell full of seawater wins."

Jack agreed. Speedwell untied his leg, and the two racers lined up. "May the best one win," Jack said, and shot off the starter gun—*bang!*

They were off in a cloud of dust.

One thing you have to remember about witches is they don't play by the rules; they'll cheat every chance they get. This time was no different.

Speedwell ran to the ocean, filled up his eggshell, and was three-quarters back when Mourning Belle saw him coming. "Stop, Speedwell!" she called. "There's no point in me going any farther; you've won for sure. Set down and let an old lady catch her breath."

Speedwell felt sorry for her and sat down, holding his eggshell full of seawater. Quicker than you could say "Jack Robinson" she threw a spell on Speedwell. He just keeled over asleep, and to keep him there, she witched the skull of a cow that she found and put it under his head like a pillow. She smashed his eggshell and set off running for the sea.

Back at the witch's house, Harkwell cocked his ear and said, "Hark, I can hear someone snoring, and it sounds like Speedwell."

Seewell stood up, shaded his eyes, and said, "Lordy, it is Speedwell. He's sleeping with a cow's skull under his head. His eggshell's smashed, and Mourning Belle's footprints are all around him."

"Ay, law," moaned Jack, "if she wins, we'll all be dead, or working for her, which is about as bad."

"Don't forget about me!" said Shootwell. He got up on the witch's stump, took aim, and shot that cow's skull right out from under Speedwell's head.

You can believe that woke him up quick! He saw what had happened, raced back to the henhouse, got another egg, and took off for the ocean again. He filled it and was back a good half hour before Mourning Belle.

She raced up puffing, sure that she'd won Jack's ship and crew. She was fit to be tied when she saw Speedwell there. "How do I know that's really seawater? Here. Let me taste it."

Jack held the eggshell for her, and they both tasted it. Then all the others did the same.

"Ye've won this time, Jack, though I can't figure out how ye done it unless Old Graybeard helped ye out."

"How I did it is no business of yours, ma'am," said Jack. "Now tell me how to get the spell off the princess."

Mourning Belle rummaged around in her pocket and

pulled out a little bottle. "This is magic water, Jack. If you just sprinkle some of this on the girl, the spell will be off."

Jack and his crew got back in the ship and set sail for the king's palace.

This time Mourning Belle was good as her word. Soon as Jack sprinkled the magic water on the princess, she jumped up, combed her hair, put on a pretty dress, and said that she felt like dancing. Anyone could see she was cured!

Jack and the king's girl liked each other, but she was stuck on some feller in the king's guard. Jack said that was fine, because he wanted some more adventures before he settled down. The king gave Jack and his crew a sack of gold apiece as a reward.

They took the ship back to Jack's home and let him off. He said the crew could take it and go adventuring where they could find enough to eat and drink and all. The countryside in these parts couldn't very well support such fellers.

One of the first things Jack did when he got back was to pay Old Graybeard the hundred dollars he owed him.

Every once in a while Jack would get a hankering to see his ship and would give a shout. Harkwell would hear him, and in a while there it would be, hovering above Jack's head. He took me riding on it when I was just a girl. In those days there wasn't anything else in the sky. These days, with all the private planes and hang gliders in the mountains, no one would pay it any mind.

Jack of Hearts
and King Marock

o one knows for sure who King Marock was. But my old Scottish granddaddy told me he was the Green Man o' Knowledge and that he came from east of the sun and west of the stars.

This story happened when Jack was twenty-one. He was a handsome strappin' feller and just itchin' to be off seekin' his fortune. His maw didn't want him to go, for it was a wild time abroad with wars goin' on an' sich, and like most mothers, she was protective of her child. But Jack got up early one morning and snuck off while she was still asleep. There was precious little food in the house, and

Jack didn't want his maw to go hungry, so he left with nary a bite of breakfast.

He come to a fork in the road he hadn't seen before. "Bedad," he said, "if I'm seekin' my fortune, I may as well go where I've never been before." So he took that turn and walked all morning, dreaming of what he might find ahead. Toward lunchtime, though, he was gettin' mighty hungry and thirsty. When he saw a mossy horse trough by the road, he headed toward it.

"At least I can get a drink," he said, flinging himself down. He had a long drink and splashed water over his head to clear away the dust of the road.

"Travelin' is hot work, ay, Jack?" said a teensy voice. Jack looked around. No one was there, but a little robin stood cockin' its head at him.

"Law, birdie, was it you talking to me?" asked Jack.

"Ay, Jack, why do ye look so surprised?"

Jack scratched his chin and thought about it. "I never heared tell of a talking bird."

"If ye wanted it to be like home, ye shouldn'ta left there," the bird answered.

"I'm off to seek my fortune," said Jack, "but right now things look worse than ever, for I'm might nigh starvin'."

"Well, ye've come to the right place," said the robin. "There's an inn over yonder hill where ye can get a meal and a game of cards."

"That won't help much. I've got no money for either one."

"It so happens," said the robin, "that someone was expecting you. Reach down under the waterspout; there's a golden guinea been waiting for you these twenty-one years."

Sure enough, Jack found the gold coin, and he thanked the bird and set off for the inn. It was over the hill, where the bird said it would be. There were three fine horses standing outside, smoke coming from the chimney, and a smell of food drifting out that almost knocked him over.

He walked inside and over to where four men were playing cards. They were Old King Marock, the innkeeper, and two of Marock's men.

"Who is this, the knave of hearts?" The king laughed. "Thunderation, boy, get yourself something to eat. I can't think with your stomach rumbling on like that."

Jack was happy to oblige. He had some of the king's grub while he watched the card game. Marock had a stack of money in front of him, so Jack could see he was winning. After a while one of the men folded, and the king turned to Jack. "Come join us. I'm not of a mind to stop now."

"I don't have much money," said Jack. "Only this gold guinea."

The king smiled at him, kind of slylike. "Don't poor-mouth me; that's enough to get ye in."

So Jack pulled up a chair and joined the game. Old Marock beat him seven times; Jack still had a little money left, and by now he was warmed up, so they started in to playin' again. This time Jack beat Marock six times straight and cleaned him out. So the king bet Jack one of his daughters against the stack of money.

Jack won again, but before he could lay down his cards, Old King Marock and every bit of money suddenly disappeared. Jack was pretty sore. "That's no way to treat a young feller alone in the world!" he protested.

Jack asked the landlord if he knew where the king had gone.

"Oh, no, Jack," he said. "No one around here is fool enough to go lookin' for him. They say he's some kind of wizard. No tellin' what sort of trouble you'd find at his place."

But Marock owed him a pile of money, and his daughter besides, so Jack wheedled till the landlord give in. "Go up the road apiece and ask Old Man Freezewell. He's the only one might know."

Jack went up the road till he come to a house with icicles hangin' all over, while hit was warm as summer everywhere else. Old Man Freezewell was settin' on the porch, his breath comin' out all icy.

Jack went up and set with him awhile and told him what King Marock had done to him.

"Ay, law, he's a rogue all right. He never makes good on his promises."

Jack hung around and helped with the chores. Old Man Freezewell took a shine to him. "Look here, Jack," he said that evening, "I like a young feller with your kind of spunk. I'll do what I can to help ye. You stay here and get a good night's sleep, and I'll see if I can freeze Marock out."

So Jack went to sleep, and when he woke up in the morning, everything outside was froze up solid. Jack and Freezewell had them a good breakfast of coffee, grits, eggs, and sausages.

"I didn't find Marock, Jack. But I found an old man knows where his girls go to bathe. Now this man's mad at me, 'cause I froze up his beer last night. Here's a little rod will thaw it out for him. His name is Brewer. Whyn't ye jest go on up and pay him a visit?"

Jack left right after breakfast for Old Man Brewer's place. He was outside choppin' wood and just a-cussin'.

"Howdy, Mr. Brewer," said Jack, right casual. "I hear ye got some beer to sell to a travelin' man."

Old Brewer stopped and wiped his forred with a handkerchief. "Well, ye heared wrong, young feller! Freezewell froze everything up last night for some blame-fool reason. Every keg of beer I've got is froze solid. It'll be the ruination of me!"

"Oh," said Jack, "is that all? I've got me here a little magic rod that can fix that. Show me the beer."

Jack touched each keg with the rod. Lo and behold, they thawed, just like that!

So Jack set with Old Brewer awhile and told him the story.

"Marock is a bad un to cheat ye, Jack. But my hat's off to anyone can beat that Old Scratch in cards. If you do like I tell ye, I think you could collect your winnings. Marock's two older girls is as bad as their daddy. But the youngest one would make ye a fine wife. What ye need to do is go along to the place where they bathe on a Saturday. They will take off all their clothes, and when they're start nekked they turn into swans and swim out on the water. The two oldest girls will come first. They'll turn into black swans. The last one will come down to the water by herself, and she'll turn into a little white swan. Now you watch where she puts all her clothes, and you pick up ever' single thing—ribbons, hairpins, and all. If you leave airy thing, she's so clever she can turn it into a whole outfit, and you'll lose out.

"When she comes out of the water, don't you give her clothes back till she promises to take you to her daddy's house. You'd never get there on your own."

The next day was Saturday. Jack thanked Old Brewer and set out. He found the spot by the river and lay up out of sight where he could see all that went on. The two older girls came first, like Mr. Brewer said they would. They took off their clothes, turned into black swans, and swam away.

Then the youngest girl came tripping down to the river. Now Jack was right taken with her soon as he saw her. He watched where she put her dress and petticoat, her sash and slippers, and even her hairpins. As soon as she turned into a white swan and swam away, Jack crept out, and gathered up ever' stitch and ever' pin.

He went back into hiding till the older sisters had come back, dressed in their clothes, and gone away.

Then the white swan come swimming back. Directly its feet touched the ground, it turned back into the beautiful girl Jack had seen before.

Then Jack stepped out of hiding, with all her clothes wrapped up in a bundle.

Well, she screamed, and looked this way and that, and pulled her long hair all around her, she was so cumfluttered to be standing there without any clothes before a strange young man.

"Oh, give me back my clothes," she pleaded, "or you're no gentleman."

"Ah, I'm no gentleman, but the poor mountain boy your father cheated at cards. They call me Jack, and what may be your name?"

"They call me Featherflight. But give me back my clothes or they will call me dead." And the girl began to cry.

Now this was hard for Jack, but he remembered Old Brewer's words, and now he was *sure* that he didn't want to lose his winnings. "I can't rightly give your clothes back unless you promise to take me to your father's house."

"Oh, I cannot do that, Jack. We'd both be killed by my father's demons. For no mortal man has ever left his house alive."

"Now that I've seen you, I'll be the *first* or die a-trying."

There was no help for it, and time was wasting, so Featherflight agreed to take Jack with her. She put on her clothes, did up her hair, and took a golden needle from her pocket. "Stick this in your shirt where it can't be seen, and hold tight to my hand."

Jack stuck the needle under his collar, took the girl's hand, and they flew up into the air as light as two feathers. The things Jack saw below told him for sure that these were not the mountains he knew.

When they come to Marock's place, the girl left him in hiding.

"You come up to the house like you got here on your own. Don't you never tell I brought you here, or it'll be the end of me."

Jack made the promise, and Featherflight flew to the house, 'cause the pink of evening was coming on and she was late for her chores.

He ambled on up to the house and banged the big brass knocker. One of the men Jack had seen in the inn opened the door. He took Jack inside, to where Marock and the girls were just settin' down to dinner.

"Howdy, Marock," said Jack.

"Howdy, Jack. How'd ye get here?" asked the king.

"Old man told me."

"Well, come on in, and pull up a chair. If you can find anything to eat, you're welcome to it." The table was covered with every good thing to eat, and Jack's mouth was just a-waterin' at the sight of it.

"You girls sure know how to cook," said Jack. "Lord, it looks good!"

Well, sir, those words were no sooner out of his mouth

The things Jack saw below told him for sure that these were not the mountains he knew.

than ever' bit of food disappeared. King Marock looked at Jack right hard, got up from the table without a word, and walked out of the room. The older sisters left, too. Feather-flight took up a taper and showed Jack to his room.

"Don't never mention the name of the Lord around here," she told him. "It kind of undoes some things. My daddy means to kill ye. But I'll save your life if I can, for I'm kinda sweet on you."

Jack's heart took a little skip when she said that, but he didn't let on.

When they got to his room, Featherflight told him, "Tomorrow Marock is going to give you a thicket to clear. He'll show you a big ax and a little rickety hatchet. Now you be sure and take the little hatchet."

But Jack was so busy lookin' at Featherflight's pretty face that he wasn't half payin' attention to what she said. I reckon men is like that sometimes.

Next morning, when Marock got up, Jack was already in the kitchen, with the fire made and coffee boilin'.

They cooked some breakfast together and sat down to eat. "Seems like you forgot to pay me my winnings," said Jack, bold as brass.

"Well, ye see, son, I can't rightly let one of my daughters go to just anyone. I've got to know what kind of stuff you're made of. You can understand that."

"What have I got to do?" Jack asked.

"First, ye've got to clear away a thicket down by the river. My granny lost her wedding ring down there, and we never could find it. You clear away the bresh, and find the ring before nightfall, or I'll put your head on a spear and line it up with all the others who came collecting debts from me."

He took Jack down and showed him the bresh thicket. Then he gave Jack a choice. "You can have this new ax or this rickety old hatchet. Which do ye want?"

Well, Jack looked at that thicket. It was a heap of work to do before nightfall, and he figured he'd need the shiny ax to get through it. So he took the ax and started in. Ever' time he'd cut out a big hunk of the bresh, it would grow back twice as big. By lunchtime there was a regular forest growing there. Jack leaned on the ax and looked at the grinning skulls of the men who'd come before. "Reckon I'll join y'all tonight," he said to them.

He might have, too, except that Featherflight appeared at just that minute. "Ye got yourself into a mess, Jack. Why didn't ye do what I told you?"

Jack said he plumb forgot. So she handed him the little rusty hatchet. He hadn't took more than three licks with it when the whole forest disappeared. Just one little gnarled-up bush was left standing. And it had the gold ring hanging on one of its branches.

Jack put the ring on his little finger, then leaned the hatchet against the bush.

"Don't come back till nightfall, or Daddy will be suspicious," said Featherflight. "Tomorrow he's going to give you a well to empty. He'll show you a new bucket and an old riddly one. You be sure and pick the old one."

But Jack was so besotted with Featherflight that his mind was riddly, and her good advice just dribbled on through. Toward evening he rambled up to the house, carrying the new ax.

Jack handed the ring to Marock. "Some of my people must be helping ye," Marock said.

"Nobody is," said Jack.

They all had supper together and went off to bed. Next morning King Marock took Jack out and showed him an old well. "My great-granny lost her silver thimble down that well, and we never could find it. My daughter ought to have it if she's going to get married."

He showed Jack a new shiny bucket and an old riddly one. "Take whichever you want, Jack, but mind, if you don't find the thimble by nightfall, I'll have your head on a spear."

The very word *married* set Jack's heart dancing, and he clean forgot what he was supposed to do. He took the new bucket and started winding water out of the well with it. But every bucketful he poured out, seemed like two buckets come back. By twelve o'clock the water was washing over the side and pouring over Jack's feet.

Featherflight come walking up with the old bucket. "Why didn't you take this one, Jack?"

"That old leaky thing wouldn't draw nothing, woman! I had a heap of work to do here."

"Just try it, Jack." She smiled at him.

Sure enough, when Jack used the old bucket, the ground and the well were dry as a bone after three bucketfuls. They could see the thimble shinin' down at the bottom.

"Hold on to the bucket, Jack, and I'll let ye down," said Featherflight. She let Jack down to where he could reach the thimble, then wound him back up to the top. She was the least-looking little thing, but she was strong enough. Love will do that to ye sometimes. They left the bucket hanging in the well.

"Now tomorrow, you'll have the worst job of all, Jack," Featherflight told him. "The king will let ye choose between a sledgehammer and a little rock hammer to bust up a hillside. On pain of your life, remember to take the little un." But Jack stood starin' at her like a moonstruck calf and never heard a word she said.

Around dusk Jack strolled back up to the house and give Marock the thimble. Marock looked at Jack real hard. "Surely some of my people is helpin' ye."

"No, nary one of them," Jack said firmly.

They went in and ate the dinner the girls had fixed. "Better get an early bedtime tonight, Jack. I want ye up bright and early to finish your chores for me." Jack just nodded. He was too hungry to take a chance on the food disappearin' again.

Next morning King Marock took Jack out to a high rock cliff. "There's enough rock here to build you and my girl a fine house. I want ye to dress out this cliff in twelve-foot blocks and have a twelve-room house built before the sun sets. If ye don't make it, I'll have your head for sure."

He showed Jack a big sledgehammer and a little rock hammer with a busted handle and made him choose. Like before, Jack took the tool that looked like it would do the job.

79

Well, he swung that sledgehammer and bashed and banged and split till he was plumb wore-out. Ever' time he'd make a crack or two, the hill would heal right back like it was before. Come noontime, his hands were covered with blisters, and he was pantin' like an old hound dog.

Up come Featherflight with the little rock hammer. "Ye haven't got too many blocks dressed, Jack. Why didn't ye take the little hammer like I told ye?"

"Did you tell me that? I don't remember."

"Well, here, try it out," she said.

Jack hit the cliffside with that little hammer, and each time he did, there was a stack of clean, dressed blocks waiting to be used. And when there was enough of them, they just formed themselves into a rock house, grand as any hotel. Without thinking about it, Jack put the little rock hammer in his pocket.

"Tonight Daddy will come down here to see how you're doin'. You show him all around the house. He'll act real pleased that you done such a fine job. But when the two of you go outside and turn your backs on the house, it will disappear. He'll pretend you didn't build it right. You just tell him you were hired to build the house, not make it stay built."

Jack thanked her and sat down to sleep in the sun. He was that tired! 'Round sundown old Marock come to inspect Jack's work. Now he was plumb put out that the house was finished, and so fine-lookin', but he pretended to like it. They went through every room.

"It's a fine job, Jack. I couldn't have done better myself," said Marock. "I reckon we better get on back to my house. It's might nigh dinnertime."

Soon as they walked out the front door and turned their backs on the house, they heard a noise like an avalanche behind them. When they turned around, the house was gone, and the rock cliff looked just like it had before.

"Hellfire, Jack, what kind of builder are ye?" shouted Marock. "The house is already gone!"

"Well," said Jack, "you just told me to get it built. You never said nothin' about keepin' it built."

Old King Marock walked back to the house just a-grumbling. He went off to bed without any dinner. Said he had a headache.

Just like before, Featherflight showed Jack to his room. "Tomorrow he'll ask you to pick your prize. Which one of us will you choose?"

"I think ye know already I'd pick you over anybody."

"Well, if you really care for me, Jack, you'll remember what I tell ye this time."

Jack promised he would.

"We'll all be swans tomorrow, and just to fool you, my feathers will be black like my sisters'. When he asks you to choose, I'll bob my head three times so you'll know me."

Next mornin' Marock sent for Jack to come to him double quick.

Jack found him by the river, and there was three swans swimming on the water. All three of them were black as the ace of spades.

"Choose, Jack, choose the girl you want, or I'll cut off your head!" shouted Old Marock. Featherflight nodded her head three times so Jack would know her.

"I'll choose this one," said Jack, pointing her out. Sure enough, when the girls changed back into their human shapes, his sweetheart stood before him.

"I don't know how ye done it," said Marock. "But ye done beat me again. Ye'll have to wait till tomorrow to leave, though, 'cause I've got to get your money together, and she has to pack her things."

Since ever'thing was settled, Jack and Featherflight got to spend some time walking around in the moonlight. Jack finally told her how he felt about her, and it looked like things were going to have a happy ending. But that was figuring without the two older sisters. They were jealous that Featherflight was going away to the mortal world with her sweetheart. They begrudged her that, and so they went to their father and told him they had seen Featherflight helping Jack.

After bedtime Featherflight ran to Jack's room and knocked on the door. He let her in, and she was shiverin' like an aspen in the wind. "Oh, Jack, my daddy has found out that I helped you, and he aims to kill us both. I heard him callin' up his demons."

"Then we'll have to fly away," said Jack.

"I can't fly anymore, Jack. My love for mortal man has taken that power away."

"Is there another way out of here?" Jack was gettin' a little bit anxious.

"Yes. You sneak down to the stable and lead out the oldest mule and the skinniest horse. Pass all the good ones by. I'll get the harness and meet you there."

By now Jack had learned to listen and remember what he was told. He snuck down to the stable and found an old mule with his nose in the manger, almost asleep, and a skinny horse that could hardly walk. He led them out of their stables. Featherflight was coming with the harness and saddles.

"I'll saddle them," said Jack.

"No, I will," said his sweetheart. "For I know the trick to it." She flung the saddles on and tightened them. Quick as *that* those two sorry animals turned into fine sleek mounts. Jack and Featherflight jumped into the saddles and were away. And it was not a minute too soon. They could hear Old Marock and his men just cuttin' the dust.

"I can't look back, for he'll witch me if I do," said Featherflight. "You'll have to watch and tell me when he's close."

Finally Jack called out, "He's right behind us now!"

Featherflight pulled a magic thorn out of her pocket and threw it back over her left shoulder. Soon as it hit the ground, it turned into a thicket of thorn trees, holly bushes, and blackberry vines so thick a rabbit couldn't get through. King Marock had to rein up his horse and go back for the rickety little hatchet.

But before he did, he shouted, "I'll get you, Featherflight. You'll be sorry you ever crossed me!"

Featherflight's heart was in her throat. She knew how

wicked her daddy could be when he was mean mad. She pushed the horse as hard as it could go, and they got a little bit ahead.

Featherflight gave Jack a little vial of water. "When he gets that close again, throw this water behind us," she said. Pretty soon they could see Old Marock just burning up the road behind them. Jack threw the vial. A great river rose up between them and the king. He had to go back after that riddly old bucket.

Next Featherflight give Jack a handful of gravel. "When he gets close this time, throw the gravel behind us." 'Bout the time they got to the inn, Marock was comin' up behind them again.

Jack done as she said, and a whole mountain grew up between them and Marock.

Marock had to turn back again to find the little rock hammer. But it was in Jack's pocket, and he never did find it. So Jack and the girl made it back to Jack's house. They could see by the horses in the pasture that Jack's paw and brothers had come home.

Jack was all for taking Featherflight in to meet his folks, but she said, "You go on in first and tell them what happened while ye were away. But don't let any of them kiss ye on the mouth, for if ye do, you'll forget about me and everything that happened in my country."

Jack said he'd never do that, and he went on in the house. There was lots of huggin' all around, but Jack wouldn't let anyone kiss him. 'Bout that time, though, Jack's little hound come running in to see him, and when he reached down to pet her, she jumped up and licked him on the mouth. Soon as she did, Jack forgot all about Featherflight and the things that happened at Marock's house.

Featherflight waited around for him to come back, but he never did. She'd seen enough of Jack to know that he weren't too swift at takin' instructions. She was feelin' tired and thirsty, so she wandered over to a little pond she could see down the road. She washed herself up and rested a spell. But then she heard someone a-comin'. Since she didn't know anybody thereabouts, she climbed up into a tree by the water and hid there.

It was a farmer's daughter coming to pick some blackberries that was growin' there. As she was pickin', she happened to look down in the water and saw Featherflight's reflection. She thought it was her own.

"Lordy, if I'm that pretty, I don't need to be hanging around here doing chores. I'll head out for the settlement and find me a beau." She left her berry bucket and went off.

The farmer's wife got tired of waitin' for the blackberries, and she come after a while to see what happened to her daughter. She saw the bucket by the water. "That good-for-nothin' has gone off gollylaggin' somewhere," she said, but when she saw Featherflight's face in the water, she thought it was her own.

"Lord a Massy. If I'm that pretty, I don't need to be waiting on that ugly old man night and day. I'll go off and find me a new husband." So she dropped her bucket and was off.

After a while the old man come in from the field. Instead of a nice hot dinner with a blackberry pie like he was expectin', he found a cold kitchen and everybody gone. So he wandered down to the blackberry thicket to see where his wife and daughter might be. There were the two buckets by the water. He bent down to pick them up and saw Featherflight's reflection. He knew he wasn't seein' his own face, so he looked up. He was plumb ugly, but he warn't stupid.

"Howdy, young lady, what ye doin' up there?"

"I'm new around here and kind of shy about meetin' folks," she answered.

"Well, come on down, I won't hurt ye. Have ye seen my wife and daughter?"

"Well, there was a young woman and an old one in a poke bonnet and apron came here and threw down their buckets. They said something about goin' to the settlement."

"Well, that's a fine howdy-do. I been workin' in the field all day, and my womenfolks done run off without makin' me any dinner. Can ye make a blackberry pie?"

"Nothin' to it," she said. She seen the old man didn't mean her no harm, so she went back and fixed him a good dinner. Next day his womenfolks were back, lookin' right sheepish, and they all had a good laugh over what happened. It was puttin'-up time, and they could use an extra hand in the kitchen, helpin' with the chores. Featherflight needed a place to live, so she stayed with the farmer's family.

Jack's folks got to pesterin' him about gettin' out on his own and gettin' married. His maw started askin' one of his old sweethearts around, and pretty soon they had set a date.

Featherflight heard about the wedding and knew for sure that Jack didn't remember her. She went out, found a little banty rooster and hen, and said some words over them. Then she filled her pocket with corn and carried the chickens to the wedding.

Jack and the girl were just standing up before the preacher when Featherflight got there. She put the chickens on the floor and threw down some corn. The hen started eatin' it, and the rooster pecked the hen on the head.

"*Squark*," screamed the hen. "Take care, my fine fellow. You don't remember the time I cleared the thicket for you and stopped King Marock with a bramble forest."

Everyone turned around to look. Jack tried to see what the commotion was, but the girl punched his arm to go on with the ceremony.

Featherflight threw down more corn. The hen pecked the corn, and the rooster pecked the hen.

"Take care, my good fellow," scolded the hen. "Don't you remember the time I dreened a well for you and stopped Marock with a river?"

Jack tried to see again, but the preacher went right on.

Everyone else was looking around at the pretty girl with the two banty chickens.

She threw down more corn. The hen ate; the rooster pecked.

"Remember, my love," said the hen, "the time I built a house for you and helped you escape from Marock for good?"

By this time everyone had crowded around Featherflight—even Jack, the girl, and the preacher. The third time the hen spoke, Jack remembered everything.

He took Featherflight by the hand, and the preacher married them on the spot. The other girl was some put out. But she forgave Jack when she heard that he had a previous engagement.

Some folks will tell you that Old King Marock is the devil himself. But Featherflight didn't have none of his mean ways. Some of her magic come in handy over the years, and after a while Jack even got so he would listen to her and remember what she said. He had to admit that sometimes she had a heap more sense than he did, and it seems as though that's a hard thing for menfolks to learn.

Muncimeg
and the Giant

t's a sure thing that Jack would have made it out of King Marock's house a whole lot sooner if he'd of listened right to Feather-flight. We women do just as well at earning our fortunes as any man can do, and sometimes we do it a whole lot better.

One of the girl stories I like is about Muncimeg and her two sisters, Polly and Nancy. Their mother took sick and was real bad off. She called her three girls in to her bedside, and she said, "I can tell I won't be around here by morning. Polly, you're the oldest, so I'm going to give you the house and garden. Nancy, you're the next oldest,

so you can have the rest of my land. As for you, Muncimeg, you can have my little pocket penknife and my gold
ring."

"Law me, Mommy. How can I make out in the world with
just your pocket penknife and gold ring?" cried Muncimeg.

"You just keep them," said her mother. "They'll come
in handy when you're in trouble." Then she turned her
face to the wall and died.

A few days after the funeral Polly and Nancy decided to
go off on their own and seek their fortunes.

"What will we do with Muncimeg?" Polly asked.

"Oh, she's such a whiny thing," said Nancy, "we'll lock
her up in the house." Now they both knew that Muncimeg
was prettier than either one of them, with her big brown
eyes and her long silky braids. They figured they'd make
out better without her along.

So they slipped out of the house, bolted the door, and
locked the shutters. Muncimeg heard the noise of the bolt
being thrown and ran to follow them. She saw them out
the winder, going off with their little traveling bags.

She tried every which way to get out, but she was locked
in tight. She sat down and cried her heart out. "Lord a
Massy and sister love, my pocket penknife and my mommy's
gold ring!" The words were no sooner out of her mouth
than the door flew wide open.

Nancy and Polly hadn't got no farther than the root cellar
under the hill when they heard Muncimeg coming.

90

"Well, dadgummit, here she comes already! What are we going to do with that little pest now?" asked Polly.

"Let's lock her in the root cellar," said Nancy. So they locked her in the root cellar, rolled some big rocks in front of the door, and took off down the road.

Muncimeg waited awhile to see if they were coming back for her. Then she sat down and cried, "Lord a Massy and sister love, my pocket penknife and my mommy's gold ring!"

The rocks rolled away, and the root-cellar door flew open.

Muncimeg followed on behind her sisters and caught up with them just as they was settin' down to have their lunch. They weren't too happy to see her, but they didn't let on. Nancy saw a holler tree nearby and give Polly a sign. They threw Muncimeg down in that holler tree and stopped it up with heavy logs and sich so she couldn't get out.

This was the worst fix she'd been in yet, and Muncimeg wailed, "Lord a Massy and sister love, my pocket penknife and my mommy's gold ring!" The heavy logs and bresh flew out, and she climbed up and got free.

By now her sisters were gettin' into some strange country, and there was nowhere to lock Muncimeg up. Besides that, dark was coming on. It was gettin' kind of spooky, with bats flying and owls *hoohoo*ing. They were right glad for the extra company. So they all three traveled on together.

After a while they could see a fine house up ahead.

They could just make out the name on the mailbox: I. Munchwell.

"Must be some kind of doctor's house; it's big enough," said Muncimeg.

Polly and Nancy were too skeered to knock, but Muncimeg went bold as brass and banged on the door. A great big girl come and opened the door.

She smiled at them. "Come on in. Travelers are *always* welcome at this house." Polly and Nancy were right glad to be invited in out of the night air.

Well, it turned out that the girl had two sisters who were just about as big as she was. After dinner the six girls sat down and played some games together and got on like a house afire.

There were lots of big knives hanging on the wall, so Polly, Nancy, and Muncimeg decided they were right about Mr. Munchwell being a doctor. But it did bother Muncimeg some that all the people in the family were such giants and had such big sharp teeth and funny yellow eyes.

Still, her sisters said, "Pay no mind. They ain't so different—jest big, that's all."

After a while it was time to go to bed. The daddy giant and his wife showed them into the bedroom where their own girls slept, side by side in one bed. "This other bed will do for you-uns," said the giant's wife to the guests.

Polly and Nancy were so tired that they went off to sleep straight away. But Muncimeg just couldn't get to sleep. After a while she could hear a moaning honing noise that she didn't like at all, so she crept out of bed and followed the sound.

It was coming from the kitchen. The old daddy giant was setting there honing a butcher knife. The whetstone moaned and groaned as it turned. His wife was cutting up onions, potatoes, and carrots in a big stewpot.

"Wifemate, how can I tell those strange girls from ourn in the dark?" he asked her.

"That's easy," said the old giant woman. "Our young-uns are all wearing nightcaps. Those strangers ain't got nary a one."

Muncimeg ran back to the room and switched the nightcaps from the giants' girls to the heads of her sisters and herself.

Sure enough, it wasn't long before that old giant come creeping in. He felt the nightcaps on Muncimeg and her sisters. Then he tippytoed over to the other bed and felt the bare heads of his daughters. Without a sound, he cut all three of their throats and went to bed, thinking of the fine meal they'd have the next day.

Muncimeg waited till it was light. Then she woke up her two sisters. When they saw what was in the other bed, they really cut the dust gettin' away from there.

They were still runnin' when they got to the king's house. He sent for them and heard their story. "My hat's off to anybody can get the best of Old Munchwell. You girls are welcome here for as long as you want to stay."

Later on he called Muncimeg aside and said to her, "My

oldest son is about the same age as Polly. I'd let him marry her if you'd go back to the giant's house and get rid of his old lady."

Muncimeg didn't really want to do it, but her two sisters kept worrying and begging her till she finally agreed. So she went back and hid near the well. The old giant woman come out and leaned over to draw out some water; Muncimeg run at her and knocked her headfirst into the well. She let out a big yell on the way down, and then she sunk to the bottom like a stone, with nary a blubber.

The giant come running when he heard his wife yell, but he was too late to save her. "I'll get you for this, Muncimeg!" he shouted. "You caused me to kill my three daughters; now you've drowned my old lady." And he set off after her.

Muncimeg got to a river. It was too wide for her to get across, and Munchweli was coming at her lickety-split. "Lord a Massy and sister love, my pocket penknife and my mommy's gold ring!" called out Muncimeg.

And she was on the other side. She ran straight to the king's house, and he was right glad to see her. They had a wedding the next day for Polly and his oldest son. It wasn't too long, though, till the king come looking for Muncimeg again.

"Your sister Nancy and my next son would make a good pair. I'll let them get married if you'll get me the giant's horse. His blanket is covered with gold bells, so you'll have to be careful getting him out." Muncimeg sure didn't want to see that old giant again, but Nancy kept naggin' till she gave in.

Muncimeg didn't have no trouble getting the horse saddled and bridled, but when she got on him and started riding away, the bells commenced to rattling and ringing. The old giant heard the bells and run out after her. She spurred the horse on, but he was gaining on her, so Muncimeg whispered, "Lord a Massy and sister love, my pocket penknife and my mommy's gold ring!" She became a teeny thing and hid in the horse's ear. The giant caught the horse and led him back to his stable.

Muncimeg waited till she thought the giant might be asleep and tried again. This time she walked the horse to the edge of the pasture before she started riding. It wasn't far enough, though, because Munchwell heard her again. Once more she became a teeny thing, but this time she hid under the horse's mane. And Munchwell led the horse back to the barn.

The third time she led the horse almost to the river. By the time Munchwell heard her it was too late. He roared out after her, "I'll get you, Muncimeg! You made me kill my daughters, you drowned my old lady, and now you stole my horse."

But Muncimeg shouted, "Lord a Massy and sister love, my pocket penknife and my mommy's gold ring!" She and the horse jumped over the water just a-jingling and were at the king's house in no time. Everyone was glad to see her, and there was a wedding the next day.

The king's youngest son took to following Muncimeg around, and everyone could see that she liked him, too. The king finally said to her, "You and my son could get married if you'd bring me the sack of gold the giant keeps under his pillow." Muncimeg didn't much want to go again, but everyone kept pestering her. And there was something in that girl that made her want adventure as much as any man.

So she went back one last time. By now the giant was fast asleep in his bed. She managed to wiggle the gold out from under his head, but he heard her on the way down the squeaky stairs and caught her. He put her in a sack and said, "I told you I'd get you, Muncimeg. You made me kill my daughters, you drowned my old lady, you stole my horse, and now you're trying to steal my gold. I'm going to get my frail and beat you till your bones crack like china."

When he went to get his frail, she said, "Lord a Massy and sister love, my pocket penknife and my mommy's gold ring!" and she was out of that sack quick as she finished. She gathered up all the dishes and china she could find, put them in the sack, and tied it back up. Then she hid behind the dresser. The giant come back. Every time he hit the sack, the china would crack and she would scream, so the giant thought she was still inside. After a while, though, she picked up the gold and lit out for the king's palace. The giant was having so much fun he never saw her go, and she got back safe and sound.

So there was one more wedding. Her sisters and their

She managed to wiggle the gold out from under his head.

husbands went back home, but Muncimeg and her husband had all the giant's gold, so they stayed in the king's house and ruled that county.

Muncimeg was not only pretty and brave but smart about helping other folks out of trouble, too. And no matter what new law she thought up, she let her husband think it was his idea all along, which makes her a pretty smart gal, doing so well for herself out in the world.

Jack and Old Raggedy Bones

ack was never afeard of nothing, and this story shows just what a reckless feller he was. It happened when he was a middle-aged man just coming home from the wars. He'd been away for twenty year or more.

In those days, when they let you off from the army, they didn't give you any kind of pay—just two loaves of white bread. So that was all he had except for his army swoard and his wore-out uniform. He was heading for home up a mountain road when he met a skinny beggar.

"Oh, soldier, can ye help a pore old man? Times have

been hard, and I've got no family to look after me. I'm might nigh starving."

Jack had a kind heart, and the man was pitiful, so Jack gave him a loaf of his bread.

It wasn't half a mile up the road that he met another ragged old man. This one was leaning on a staff, and he had a gray beard halfway down to his knees.

"Howdy, soldier, can ye help me out? I haven't eaten in days. I'm plumb sick with hunger."

"I haven't got much, Granddaddy. But I'll share my loaf of bread with ye." Jack unwrapped the loaf, cut it in two, and gave the man half of it. He went on up the road toward home, but he hadn't got far when he started thinking that he hadn't been fair to the second old man, so he turned around and ran down the road till he caught up with him.

"Hey, Graybeard, wait up. I give a whole loaf of bread to another hungry man, and I only give you a half. So here's the other half I cheated you out of."

Old Graybeard kind of rared back and straightened up.

"Well, Jack, good company shortens the road. Whyn't ye jest set down and share a bite with me before you travel on?"

"Thankee, Graybeard, I could go farther and fare worse," said Jack, who *was* feeling a mite hungry.

But when the old man unwrapped the half loaf, there were other good things to eat alongside it—slabs of country ham, cold chicken, and a bottle of sweet milk besides.

"Blow me down," said Jack, "where did all that come from?"

"Some days it's either feast or famine," Graybeard chuckled. "And besides, never look a gift horse in the mouth."

So Jack and Graybeard sat and ate and exchanged a few stories about what had gone on while Jack was away. Mountain folks had it hard with so many young men away fighting.

When it was time to part ways, Graybeard took something out of his pocket.

"You're a good man, Jack, and they're hard to find in this world. I'm going to give you two things that'll help ye get back on your feet."

He unrolled a sack made out of the finest leather, with some strange writing and designs on it. "Hold this sack open, and whack it with your hand, and say:

> "*Whickety whack, ———,*
> *Get into my sack!*

"Name the thing you want to get in there, and it will have to do as you say, no matter how big or strong it is."

From his waistcoat pocket he pulled a rainbow-colored bottle. "This is a foretelling jar. It will tell you whether someone is going to live or die. All you have to do is fill it with clear springwater, and set it right still by a sick person's bed. After a while blubbers will form in the bottle; if they rise to the top, that person is going to live, but if they sink to the bottom, that poor soul is going to die for sure. And if you hold it up and look through it, you'll see Old Man Death himself, standing by the left of that person's head."

"Thank you, Granddaddy," said Jack. "I hope to see you again."

"Don't mention it, son. Good luck to ye always, and remember—don't take no wooden nickels." And he skipped off down the road, chuckling to himself.

Jack continued on toward home.

By the time dusk was falling, Jack was getting footsore and weary. He stopped by the road to rest, and he heard the *gobble-gobble* of wild turkeys nesting for the night. He crept toward the sound, and sure enough, he come to a tree where seven large turkeys were singing themselves to sleep. Very quietly Jack took out his sack, held it open, gave it a whack, and shouted:

> *"Whickety whack, turkeys,*
> *Get into my sack!"*

Well, sir, all seven of those turkeys flew down into Jack's sack one after the other. He tied it up with a piece of rope. Funny thing was, the sack didn't seem no heavier than it had been before. Jack walked on till it was plumb dark. He was tired and hungry and thinking about cooking one of those turkeys when he saw a light up ahead.

'Round a bend in the road he come to a little country inn. There were horses and carriages out front. The smell of food and the sound of music drifted out and settled all around him. He went 'round to the back and asked for the innkeeper.

A well-fed man came out, wiping his hands on his apron.

"Howdy, Mr. Innkeeper," said Jack. "I've just come back from the wars, and I've got no money. Would ye swap me a meal and a bed for seven wild turkeys?"

"Sounds fair to me," said the man. "Where are they?"

Jack opened the sack and pulled out the first one. It was a fine big bird. The innkeeper looked at Jack kind of queerlike; the turkey was bigger than the sack.

"If they're all as good as this, I'll throw in a hot bath and three dollars besides, soldier."

Well, it seemed like each turkey Jack pulled out was bigger than the one before it, and he kept on till all seven birds tied by the feet were lying there. The innkeeper give Jack three dollars and took him in to eat his fill of good food.

Jack set off the next day feeling clean and rested, with money in his pocket besides. It had been a long time since he'd felt so good.

By and by he came to a fence running down the side of the road. It was overgrown with brambles and weeds. But behind it he could see a big house almost covered by trees and bushes. Its curtains hung in tatters, and the windows hadn't been washed in a long time.

Jack got to figurin' on it, and after a while he met a boy drivin' sheep. "Howdy, son. What can ye tell me about that empty house down the road apiece?"

The boy looked kind of scaredlike. "Law, mister," he said, "it's full of haints—belongs to Old Obidiah Jones. He lives in the next house along the road." The boy skedaddled on as if he didn't want to talk about it anymore.

When Jack come to the next house, it looked just like the empty one except that it was fixed up pretty, with fresh curtains and a white coat of paint. It had flowers around it, and livestock grazed in the fields. Jack went up to the door and banged the brass knocker.

A pretty white-haired old lady come to the door. "What can I do for ye, soldier?" she asked.

Jack took off his hat. "I'd like to talk to your husband, please, ma'am."

She took him in to where Obidiah was just about to eat his lunch.

"Come on in and have a bite, stranger," he said. He was eager to hear about the war and the outside world, him being old and not able to get around much.

Jack told him about his adventures and then helped out with the chores. In the afternoon they sat on the porch having lemonade and cookies.

"Obidiah, what about that empty house you got down the road?" said Jack.

"Bedad," said the old man, "that house has been hainted for over forty years. Something kills every soul who tries to spend a night in it. Why, I'd give that house and a hundred acres around it to anyone who could make it safe. It's been an eyesore and a blight on the whole community."

Jack studied on it awhile. "I been away for twenty year or more—don't reckon I'm going home to much. I'll give it a try."

"I'd sure like to have ye for a neighbor, Jack, but I'd hate to see ye dead like them others that spent the night up there."

But Jack was determined to try it, so they gave him the key. Obidiah's wife packed a skillet and some vittles in a poke, and he set off for the house before nightfall.

He turned the key and pushed the door open. It creaked on its hinges. Spiderwebs hung everywhere. The inside was dark, but Jack could see little hoofprints in the dust all around the fireplace.

Jack scratched his head. "Looks like someone's little goat has been playin' around here. Wonder how it got in."

He chopped some wood and made a big fire in the fireplace. He swept the floor clean and laid out his bedroll and vittles so it looked right cozy. He took off his swoard and laid it where he could reach it. He cooked his dinner and et it and sat by the fire, musing as the dark came on.

"Reckon them haints don't aim to show up," he said. The words were no sooner out of his mouth than he heard a commotion up the chimbly. Such a rattling and banging and screeching you never heard in all your borned days.

Then out of the fireplace flew three little devils, coughing and red-eyed from the smoke and soot. Their horns and fangs shone golden in the firelight. Every one of them carried a swoard and a sack of money.

"Howdy, Jack," they squealed. "Mind if we sit here and play a little game of cards?"

"Why not? Won't bother me none." Jack smoked his pipe and pretended to whittle a piece of wood. But he was really studying the way they played their hands. They were playing blackjack, and the stakes was high.

"Come on and play with us. Four-hand is better than three-," they wheedled.

"I ain't much of a card-playin' man," Jack lied. "And besides, all I've got in the world is three dollars."

"We ain't prejudiced, come on and play."

Finally Jack agreed and joined in their game. He started right in to winning—first from one, then another. The little devils started getting peevy with Jack, and walking over to the fire to light their pipes, trying to see his hand. But Jack played close to his chest.

It wasn't long till he'd won every bit of money they had. Them little devils was mad as hornets. They flew all around Jack, slashing with their swoards and ready to take a bite out of him if they could get close enough. It was clear they meant to kill him like they done the others.

Jack swung his army swoard around him and fought them off as well as he could, but it didn't take long for him to get wore-out fighting three devils at once. He was starting to get scared when he remembered the sack Graybeard had given him. He snatched it out of his pocket, helt it open, and shouted:

"Whickety whack, devils,
Get into my sack!"

Those little devils stopped in midair and flew into Jack's sack without a whimper. Jack tied up the mouth of the sack. Then he unrolled his bed pack and went off to sleep. It had been a long day.

In the morning Mr. Jones came to see how Jack had fared. He brought along his shovel to bury the remains if he needed to. Jack sat up, yawned, put on a pot of coffee, and told him all that had happened. Then they counted the money Jack had won. He was a rich man!

"Jack, I'm going to keep my bargain with ye. The house and a hundred acres is yourn to keep. There's enough money here to hire some hands to fix up your house and buy some good livestock. You don't ever have to do another lick of work if you don't want to."

"What are we going to do with these little devils?" Jack asked.

"Let's take them down to John Blacksmith. He'll know what to do with them." So they took the sack down to Old John and told him the whole story.

"Their daddy and me are kind of in the same business— fire and brimstone and all. They don't scare me a bit." So he put the sack on the anvil and pounded it with his hammer. Sparks flew out of the sack, and the devils hollered and fought to get away, but John kept on pounding till the sack was quiet and still. When they opened it, there was nothing inside but a pile of ashes. John went out and sprinkled them on his rosebushes and gave Jack his sack. Strange as it might seem, the sack was good as new.

Jack hired some people to fix up his house and bought himself some clothes fit for a country gentleman. He got a bay horse and a bluetick hound. Then he and Obidiah went off to all the fairs and shows and bought some prize animals— cows, sheep, guinea hens—whatever he fancied.

But busy hands is happy hands, and Jack took up whittlin' again. He could carve a bear or coon or hound dog so real it looked like it was breathin'. 'Cept for that, he didn't have much to do but roam around the country with his horse and dog. One day he heard the news that the king had offered a reward to anyone that could cure his girl. She was lying in bed, wasting away. And when a doctor failed to cure her, the king had his head cut off. Jack was ready for a new adventure, so he set off that very day for the king's house.

The king looked Jack up and down. "Ye don't look much like a doctor to me, but if you can cure my gal, I'll give you a thousand dollars. She's so bad off even her beau has give up on her." He took Jack in to where his daughter was lying in her big feather bed. She was thin and pale as a ghost. She looked like something the cat had drug in backward.

Jack felt her head and her pulse. "Take this little bottle and have someone fill it up with springwater," he said, and handed the bottle Graybeard had given him to the king.

The king looked right puzzled, but he did it. "Now just leave me alone in here for a while," Jack said. Everyone left, and Jack put the bottle of water on the bedside table next to the princess. Just as Graybeard had said, blubbers formed in the bottle. And they sank to the bottom.

"Uh-oh," thought Jack, "this don't look too good for the princess or my head."

He picked up the bottle and looked through it. Sure enough, standing on the left side of the girl's bed was Old Man Death himself. He had a size and a sack just the mate of Jack's. He was reaching out like he was going to grab her up that minute.

Old Raggedy Bones saw Jack looking at him through the bottom of the bottle. "Howdy, Jack. You done cheated me many times when you was a soldier. I guess you must be a pretty lucky feller."

"That's how my maw named me," said Jack, sneaking one hand around back of him to get his sack out of his back pocket.

"How come ye're here, Jack? Have ye done turned doctor?"

"I come here to try and save the king's daughter," said Jack.

"This here girl's done for, Jack. I'm fixing to tote her off to the next world."

"Now look here, Raggedy Bones, this girl's young and pretty. She ain't even started to live. It ain't fair to take her now!" Jack was gettin' het up.

"Shucks, Jack, Death ain't never fair." Old Raggedy Bones

Old Raggedy Bones saw Jack looking at him
through the bottom of the bottle.

started to laugh, and his shoulders started to shake, and all the things clinging to his clothes started to quiver and tinkle and dance. He was covered all over with rags and tags, snigs and snags, bones and stones, rust and dust, splinters and winters that had got stuck to him as he shoved things into that old sack.

"Everything's got to die, Jack—people, animals, trees, the moon, even the year. I take away the old wore-out things to make room for the new. I'm just doin' my job."

By this time Jack had got hold of his sack and pulled it out of his pocket. He whipped it 'round, smacked it with his hand, and said:

> *"Whickety whack, Death,*
> *Get into my sack!"*

Death piled into Jack's sack like a heap of dry bones. Quick as lightning Jack tied the mouth of the sack up with a double hitch knot to make sure he couldn't get out.

The king's daughter jumped out of bed, as spry and pretty as anything. They went out to where the king was waiting. She threw her arms around the king and Jack and everyone else. The king threw a party that night and invited everyone to come and see that his girl was well again. Her beau was there, and he was so glad to see her feeling good again that they set a wedding day right there on the spot.

The next day Jack took his thousand-dollar reward and

the sack with Death in it back to his farm. He climbed up a poplar tree and tied the sack to one of the highest branches.

The neighborhood kids liked to visit Jack, so he got out his Jack knife and started carving toys for them. He invented the Jumping Jack, the Limber Jack, the Jack-in-a-Box, and Jackstones. He carved slingshots for the boys and dolls for the girls. He made pecking chickens and jumping pigs. He got so busy thinking up new things to make that he plumb forgot about the time.

Years passed. Kids kept coming. He noticed that there were more of them than there used to be. His beard started turning white, and some cold mornings it was a little hard for him to get up. But he didn't pay it much mind. He was enjoying himself.

One day Jack took a notion to walk into town to get some store-bought candy for himself and the neighborhood young-uns. Town was a lot closer than it used to be. He put some money in his pocket and set off.

Pretty soon he heard something coming, and it was making an awful racket.

Creakity crackity
Humpity hump
Drigity dragity
Grumpity grump.

An old lady came hobbling 'round the bend. Her nose hung down, her chin stuck up; her skin was so thin her bones were showing through; she was bent so far over, Jack couldn't see her face. When he got close to her, he bent down to take a good look. It was Miz Amelia, his old neighbor.

"Howdy-do, Miz Amelia," said Jack. "I haven't seen you for a while."

The old lady straightened up a little, her old bones creaking and groaning, till she could look Jack in the eye. Her eyes were sunk so deep in her head that you could hardly see them.

"Howdy, son," she croaked.

"How you feeling, ma'am?" He wondered when she got so old!

"Lawsy, son, I'm as bad as I can be."

"What's the matter?" asked Jack.

"Oh, I'm so tired of draggin' this old body around. It's plumb wore-out. I ache in every joint. I'd give anything to die and have done with this world."

"You mean you want to die?" asked Jack.

"Oh, Lordy, yes. I've been living on this Earth for one hundred and forty years now, and I can't see going on for another month. I have so many great-great-great-grandchildren that they're driving me plumb crazy. I just hauled my old carcass off to get away from them for a while."

"Well, why can't ye die, Granny?" asked Jack in amazement.

"Can't nobody die anymore—ain't ye heard? Some blame fool has got Death tied up in a tree. It's plumb against nature."

All of a sudden Jack remembered that Old Man Death was still tied up in a sack in his tree. He knew what he had to do. He turned right around and headed home.

There was a neighbor boy playing by his gate, and Jack said, "Son, I'll give ye all the money I've got in my pocket if you'll climb up that poplar tree and bring me the sack that's tied in it."

The boy climbed up in the poplar tree, but it took him an hour or so to find the sack. The tree had growed a lot over the years. But he did find it and bring it down. Jack gave him the money and took the sack. It was covered with moss from hanging out in the weather for so long.

Jack took out his knife and carved in big letters on his door:

I've seen the world,
I've lived my fill.
I've sown my seed,
It's growing still.
Take what you want
Beyond this door,
'Cause I don't need them
ANYMORE!

Then he cut the string on the sack, and Old Death stepped out smiling and stretching and swinging his size over his head.

"Howdy, Old Raggedy Bones," said Jack.

*So Jack and Miz Amelia and the other tired old folks
who were too old to live got put in Old Death's sack.*

"Howdy, Jack," said Death. "Thankee for the rest, but I've got work to do. I reckon this time you'll go into *my* sack."

So Jack and Miz Amelia and the other tired old folks who were too old to live got put in Old Death's sack. He got a big harvest that day. But all the souls had a lot of company on the way to the next world.

Like I told you-uns in the beginning, nobody can keep Jack still and in one place for long. Not even Death. Why, just a few days ago I saw him whistlin' down the road with his hound dog at his heels and his hat pulled over his eyes. He just keeps gettin' young again. And that, young-uns, is why I'll never run out of stories to tell you. So y'all come back, ye hear?

About the Stories

Most of the stories in this collection were gathered by Poppyseed when the bean tree fell on Story Mountain. Folklorists would call them folktales, or *Märchen*—tales told by the "folk." Each contains reflections of other stories—branches and seeds of tales that grew somewhere else before taking root and then blooming in the mountains of North Carolina.

The bean tree itself may be Yggdrasil, the tree of life. It appears as regularly in folk sagas as tales of the Flood and the Creation. Taliesin, the Celtic bard, mentions the bean in his magical story of the battle between man and the evil forces of the universe. In this story the plants have taken up banner and sword on the side of man. Each plant's heroic deeds are mentioned, but of the bean it is said, "She came bringing a thousand dreams in her shadow." Indeed, it is a thousand dreams, shadows of dreams, and retellings of dreams in story form that have kept children and adults returning each night to story circles all over the world.

Stories are truly part of the Earth's heart. They have been brought up to the surface by wise men and women, story dreamers, and healers, those folk who were brave and true of heart and who risked the dangers of descent into that secret place.

Sometimes a story has the earmarks of a particular tribe or place of origin. Others are so persistent and have appeared so universally in inaccessible regions of the Earth that our hackles rise when we consider the wonder of their sameness.

Poppyseed is many grandmothers and many storytellers, but her voice is always the same. Jack, too, has had many names and faces. Sometimes his hair is as fair and straight as new corn silk, and his eyes are round and blue. At another time his hair may be curling and black, and his eyes as deep and dark as the vortex of a whirlpool. He comes from north, south, east, or west. He has many names—Hans, Ivan, Jacques, or Tecumseh—but he answers to them all.

After each full lifetime, he turns young and starts over as a lad. In some stories he wins a wife, a different one for each lifetime. As Poppyseed says, "No one can keep Jack down for long, not even Old Man Death himself."

The face of Poppyseed belongs to Ethel Thornburg Bell, who started out this life in Kings Mountain, North Carolina, the same year that the century began. She has picked cotton, put up food, made molasses, soap, and anything else her family needed. She has cradled her children and her children's children and has nurtured all the "little folks" who were given her country wisdom.

But there is still wonder in her cornflower blue eyes. She remembers relatives from Scotland, Ireland, France, and Germany, which are all places where the bean tree spread its shadow. Her neighbors on Story Mountain just down the road apiece, people of color and Native Americans, nod recognition at some of the stories off her old bean tree.

I learned my love of stories at the knee of my grandmother Ethel. I heard them with my feet planted in the red mud of North Carolina in the shadow of the mountains. They lured me off to their sources in the four corners of the world. Yet, whether I heard them in Czechoslovakia, Liechtenstein, or Istanbul, they always had echoes of home.

So I returned to the electric green and indigo blue of the North Carolina mountains, where for over ten years I have listened again to the stories of Ray Hicks, Marshall Ward, Willard Watson, and other gifted raconteurs.

The stories need retelling and translating for today's children, who have not observed the shadows of the changing seasons as they sweep across these old mountains, heard the *gee-haw* of a farmer calling to his mule, or eaten buttered corn bread fresh from the wood stove. Most of them probably wouldn't recognize a muscadine if they stepped on one barefoot. I would love to bring them all back to this land before these things disappear. I would like to let them feel what it was like to grow up observing the world from this place of wonder, where each day is young.

I would have missed many clues these stories hold without the guidance of knowledgeable friends like the late scholars A. K. Davis, in Virginia, and Cratis Williams, in Boone, North Carolina. I am indebted to many scholars, especially Charles Perdue, at the University of Virginia.

I owe much to my neighbors, like Lonnie Barlow, who have generously shared their porch swings and given me invaluable knowledge about things like the lesser and greater gommers and the elusive habits of the wild catawampus.

This is Poppyseed's word quilt, with fragments and patches collected from all over the planet Earth, sewn together with love, and big enough to shelter all you young-uns from the cold of the night air.

For my readers, I thank you for your time and trust in sharing this journey and my characters with me. You know me as well as I know you, fellow travelers off in search of another tale. For my reviewers, especially those of you who are not of the mountains, the meadows, and the streams, I hope that you find sustenance in my stories. Though their language be strange, and their world long lost to sophisticated city dwellers, there are lessons to be learned for those who can keep an open heart and mind.

About the Art

The full-page illustrations in this book were engraved on end-grain lemonwood blocks that were shipped from England.

Wood engraving has a long history in the production of books. Thomas Bewick (1753–1828) is given credit for perfecting the art of end-grain wood engraving. This technique differs from woodcuts, which are cut on the plank side of the block and thus produce a very different effect. Bewick and his school popularized wood engraving. They used boxwood, which became the primary illustrative source for books and periodicals well into the beginning of this century.

The blocks for this book were prepared by the firm of T. N. Lawrence in England. This family business is three generations old and supplied many of the blocks used by the *London Illustrated News.*

For such large publications, many small blocks were executed by a staff of engravers, and then they were bolted together to create newspaper-size illustrations of momentous events at home or in the far-flung reaches of the British Empire. And although many of these were works of art in their own right, the blocks were usually ground down to the flat wood to be used again and again.

I studied wood engraving under Charles Smith, then the chairman of the art department of the University of Virginia, who is a universally recognized printmaker and painter. From then on I was intrigued with the technique. At the Victoria and Albert Museum I was actually allowed to hold one of Bewick's blocks in my hand.

For technical help in executing and printing the book, I am indebted to Clare Leighton's textbook *Wood-engravings and Woodcuts* (London and New York: Studio Publications, 1932).

There are a handful of artists still using the technique today. But in the last two decades the wood has become scarce, and the tools are hard to find.

Wood engraving was chosen as the technique for this book because it conveys a certain nostalgic warmth reminiscent of the stories retold here. The blocks were prepared to size (clamped, glued, and sanded in three pieces for each illustration). The oversize illustrations for the cover and title page were executed with the same tools but cut on battleship linoleum.

I use an antique proof press that traveled from Virginia to London to Henley on Thames and back to North Carolina. Four strong men are required to move it—a different four men each time. And as they stretch and strain, I smile and tell them, "Moving the machinery is the easy part of storytelling. It's moving hearts and minds that is the real challenge."

Glossary

Mountain speech is old speech. It derives not from ignorance but from isolation. Many words that have been preserved here are words that were commonly used in the English language when settlers came to this country from the British Isles.

Shakespeare and Chaucer and a multitude of other writers preserve such usages in literature. Mountain people came to this country in an era when most people in Europe and Britain were preliterate. It was a time when people painted with words and preserved ideas in song and lilting ballads. It is not unusual to hear a song in the mountains that commemorates some local or historical event, such as the Battle of Culloden, which drove many Highland people from their homes and across the ocean, to settle in the highlands of America.

And because many people were fleeing famine or persecution,

they had little to bring with them except their oral tradition. The stories preserve heroic tales, cunning behavior, and humor. Though the settlers had few amusements, toys, or leisure, anyone could play with words. And so mountain speech is full of twists and turns, alliteration, simile, onomatopoeia. If there is no suitable word for something, it is not unusual to hear someone make up a new one on the spot and on command. This is obviously the way new words have always been added to the language.

We have become accustomed to the new words coined by science, politicians, economists, and the media. Mountain speech may sound quaint in today's modern homogenized world. It is, in fact, a treasure and a heritage that belongs to all English-speaking people.

Progress has made much of this language obsolete or obscure, but it still gives us clues and echoes of life in a simpler time—a time when reverence for life, work, and nature was more common and necessary than it seems today. Surely these are qualities we are learning to value again. Our high-tech throwaway society has endangered the very planet on which we live. Perhaps these stories and this language will remind us that it was not so long ago that people in our country thought, lived, and felt differently. Through the words and memories of that time we may be inspired to turn the clock back to a less hurried life, in which we may learn again to stop and play with words.

Afeard Afraid.

Airy Any or some.

Applejack Hard cider.

Ay, law Exclamation of dismay.

Banty Bantam, a miniature breed of fowl.

Beat Better.

Bedad Exclamation of surprise.

Blame Exclamation of reproach.

Blubbers Air bubbles in water.

Bresh Brush, bushes, sticks.

Brickle Brittle, easily broken.

Carousing Misbehaving, being rowdy.

Catawampus Elusive mountain animal, seen mostly by children and hermits.

Caterwampus Out of kilter, surprising.

Chimbly Chimney.

Coot Crazy old man (derogatory).

Craw Gizzard, part of a fowl in which food is ground up by stones the bird has eaten.

Critter Creature, animal.

Cudgel Club or heavy branch.

Cumfluttered Embarrassed, in a flap.

Cut the dust Go quickly down a dirt road or across a dusty field.

Dadgummit Exclamation of disappointment or dismay.

Dark of the moon New moon, night without light.

Directly Shortly or soon.

Doodly-squat Nothing, not even a tiny bit.

Draw Pull up.

Dreened Drained.

Et Ate, past tense of *eat*.

Ever' Every.

Feared of Afraid of.

Feller Fellow.

Foretelling Fortune-telling, predicting.

Forred Forehead.

Frail Whip.

Get the bead on Get in one's sights, aim for.

Gollylaggin' Courting, kissing.

Gommed it up Messed it up.

Gommer Someone who can't do anything right.

Gullet Throat, esophagus.

Hackle Comb with long iron teeth, used for straightening sheep's wool.

Hackles Standing hair, mane, feathers, fur, on back of neck.

Haints Haunts, ghosts.

Helt Held.

Het up Heated up, angry, upset.

Hit It (used for emphasis).

Holler Hollow, valley.

Iffen If.

Kilt Killed.

Law Lord.

Least Smallest, youngest; or skinny, small.

Lickety-split In a split second, quickly.

Like near Almost.

Lit into Abused, scolded, beat up.

Lit out Set out, hurried.

Lord a Massy Lord of Mercy.

'Lowed as how Allowed as how; planned, thought out, gave opinion that.

Mater Tomato.

Mess of A lot of, enough to cook a meal.

Might nigh, also *mought nigh* Nearly, almost.

Moonstruck Someone who is not in his or her right mind, dazzled by the moon, a *luna*tic.

Nary Not any, none.

Nick Slick Nick is a name for the devil, so this is rather like saying "clever devil" or "hell's bells."

Old Scratch The devil.

Ourn Ours.

Outlandish From the outlands; that is, from land or territory outside the mountain region.

Pant'er Panther, mountain lion.

Pestle tail Shaped like a pestle, with a brush at the end.

Piney woods rooter Wild piglet.

Pizen Poison.

Plumb Completely, directly.

Pocket penknife Small knife with a folding blade.

Poke Bag or sack.

Poke bonnet Bonnet that has a brim stiffened with flattened paper pokes.

Pone Corn pone, or corn bread, sometimes cooked on a hearth.

Poor-mouth To claim poverty.

Pore Poor, skinny, pitiful.

Precious little Almost none, almost gone; so what is left is valuable or precious.

Rared up Reared up on back legs; huffy or angry.

Reckon Suppose, figure, foresee.

Riddly Riddled; object full of holes, such as a colander or sieve.

Rousting Misbehaving, tearing things up.

Ruination The ruin of, disaster.

Set Sit, incubate.

Shet Shut, rid.

Sich Such.

Size Scythe.

Sizen Swinging with a scythe-like motion.

Skedaddled Ran, scampered.

Skeered Scared.

Start nekked Stark naked.

Store-bought Item bought at the store, rather than homemade.

Stove Smashed, broken in.

Strappin' Healthy, robust.

Stuck on In love with.

Swan Swoon.

Sweet milk Fresh milk, not buttermilk.

Swoard Sword. Mountain pronunciation may be the original pronunciation of the word in English, which would explain the way it is spelled.

Tail over nose So fast the back end is trying to overtake the front end.

Taper Candle.

Tetched Not quite right, crazy, tainted.

Thankee Thank ye, or thank you.

Trompin' Stomping, stamping, destroying.

Tuckered out Tired, worn-out, exhausted.

Tushes Tusks or teeth; as on a boar or ogre.

Un One.

Vittles Victuals, food.

Whimsy Amusing thing, doodad.

Whittle To carve with a knife, sometimes idly to pass the time.

Widdershins Counterclockwise; implies bewitched.

Winding water When water comes from a well, it is drawn by a pulley and a spindle, which must be cranked or wound up from below.

Witch Put a spell on.

Witched Bewitched.

Wore-out Worn-out.

Y'all Contraction of *you-all*. Contrary to popular belief outside of the South, *y'all* is used correctly only when it refers to more than one person. The exception to this rule is "Y'all come back," which may be used when one person leaves a homestead.

Young-uns Young ones, children.

Yourn Yours.

You-uns You ones, all of you.

Bibliography

Bettelheim, Bruno. *The Uses of Enchantment*. New York: Alfred A. Knopf, 1976.

Briggs, Katherine M. *A Dictionary of British Folktales in the English Language*. Bloomington: Indiana University Press, 1970.

Brown, Frank C. *North Carolina Folklore*. Durham, North Carolina: Duke University Press, 1952.

Bruford, Alan. *The Green Man of Knowledge*. Aberdeen, Scotland: Aberdeen University Press, 1982.

Campbell, Joseph. *The Hero with a Thousand Faces*. Bollingen Series. Princeton, New Jersey: Princeton University Press, 1949.

———, with Bill Moyers. *The Power of Myth*. New York: Doubleday, 1988.

Carrière, Joseph Médard. *Tales from the French Folklore of Missouri*. Evanston and Chicago: Northwestern University Press, 1937.

Chase, Richard. *The Jack Tales*. Cambridge, Massachusetts: Houghton Mifflin, 1943.

Dorson, Richard M. *The British Folklorists*. London: Routledge Kegan Paul, 1968.

———. *Peasant Customs and Savage Myths*. London: Routledge Kegan Paul, 1968. 2 vols.

Frazer, Sir J. G. *The Golden Bough*. London: Macmillan, 1911–1915.

Gerould, Gordon Hall. *The Grateful Dead: The History of a Folk Story*. Milwood, New Jersey: Kraus Reprint, 1973.

Gomme, George Laurence. *Ethnology in Folklore*. Modern Science Series. London: K. Paul, Trench, Trübner, 1892.

Haley, Gail E. Keynote Address: "Everyman Jack and the Green Man." Children's Literature Association (proceedings), University of Florida, March 1982.

———. "From the Ananse Stories to the Jack Tales: My Work with Folktales." *Children's Literature Association Quarterly*. Vol. 11, No. 3 (Fall 1986).

Jacobs, Joseph. *English Fairy Tales* and *More English Fairy Tales*. London: Bodley Head, 1968.

James, E. O. *The Tree of Life*. Leiden, Netherlands: E. J. Brill, 1966.

Jones, Gwyn and Thomas, trans. *The Mabinogion*. Netherlands: A Dragon's Dream Book, 1982.

Jung, C. G. *Memories, Dreams, Reflections*. New York: Vintage, 1967.

Keightey, Thomas. *The Fairy Mythology*. London: H. G. Bohn, 1850.

Kennedy, P. *The Fireside Stories of Ireland*. Dublin: Pa Norwood Editions, 1870.

Makay, Percy. *Tall Tales of the Kentucky Mountains*. New York: George H. Daran Co., 1924.

McGarry, Mary. *Great Family Tales of Ireland.* New York: Ariel Books, 1973.

McGowan, Thomas. "Four Beech Mountain Jack Tales." *North Carolina Folklore Society.* Vol. 26, No. 2 (September 1978).

Pearce, Joseph Chilton. *Magical Child.* New York: Bantam Books, 1977.

Perdue, Charles L. J. *Outwitting the Devil: Jack Tales from Wise County, Virginia.* Santa Fe, New Mexico: Ancient City Press, 1987.

Randolph, Vance. *Pissing in the Snow, and Other Ozark Mountain Tales.* Urbana, Chicago, London: University of Illinois Press, 1977.

Roberts, Leonard W. *Old Greasybeard Tales from the Cumberland Gap.* Detroit: Folklore Associates, 1969.

Sampson, John. *Gypsy Folk Tales.* Salem, New Hampshire: Salem House, 1984.

Squire, Charles. *Celtic Myth and Legend.* London: Gresham Publishing Co., 1901.

Stephens, James. *Irish Fairy Tales.* New York: Macmillan, 1923.

Stewig, John Warren. "Reading Pictures, Reading Texts, Some Similarities." *The New Advocate.* Vol. 5, No. 1 (Winter 1992).

Thompson, Stith, with Antti Ametus Aarne. *The Types of the Folktale: A Classification and Bibliography.* Helsinki: Suomalainen Tiedeakatemia, 1961.

The Travels of Baron Munchausen, illus. Crowquill (Doré). New York: E. P. Dutton & Co., 1923.

Zipes, Jack. *The Complete Fairy Tales of the Brothers Grimm.* New York: Bantam Books, 1987. 2 vols.

Printed in the United States
43743LVS00007B/193-216